The Commandments of God

The Commandments of God

Are They Burdensome? Are They Abolished?

Cornie Banman

iUniverse LLC
Bloomington

The Commandments of God
Are They Burdensome? Are They Abolished?

iUniverse books may be ordered through booksellers or by contacting:

iUniverse LLC
1663 Liberty Drive
Bloomington, IN 47403
www.iuniverse.com
1-800-Authors (1-800-288-4677)

ISBN: 978-1-4620-4129-9 (sc)
ISBN: 978-1-4620-4128-2 (hc)
ISBN: 978-1-4620-4321-7 (ebk)

Library of Congress Control Number: 2011913258

Printed in the United States of America

iUniverse rev. date: 07/18/2013

CONTENTS

Author Biography

I was born in a small farming community in La Crete, Alberta, Canada, in the spring of 1959. My wife, Sara Wolfe from southern Manitoba, and I got baptized in a local church in La Crete in the spring of 1981 and got married that summer. Sara has a tremendous passion for children, including the handicapped, and all children love her. She is a tremendous blessing to me and to all who know her. God blessed us with a wonderful daughter, Kathryn, in the summer of 1996. Sara is a very serious gardener for which I am truly grateful. I really enjoy studying the Holy Scriptures together with my family.

Introduction

We were raised in the Mennonite culture, which is quite an aggressive breed of people who love wealth and the luxury and technology that can be obtained by it. Our community, which consists of many wealthy people, is one of elitism and beauty, and much of the time is spent in showing that we settle for nothing but the best. Sunday mornings we have church parking lots packed with many beautiful vehicles.

After I finished eighth grade at age fifteen, I started working in the sawmill industry. I have built and maintained sawmills for other people for a few decades. I am presently employed at one that I set up in 1991 for eight local businessmen. I have usually held positions at which I was able to influence the growth and upgrading of the companies. So, needless to say, I am not exempting myself from my definition of a Mennonite. In 1997, I chose to do what I figured I was good at for myself; it was my turn to make some big money, or so I thought. I ventured into a partnership sawmill business with a long-time friend of mine who had already started on a small scale and was looking for a partner to help expand his operation. I thought I had hit the jackpot but soon learned that jackpots could be loaded with dynamite. This one was.

Business did not go as planned. I soaked our savings into the business and lost it. A few local semiretired businessmen bought the company but didn't pay for it. My life had taken a dramatic turn in a hurry, of which Satan took full advantage, and almost did get the best of me. I went down hard. I tried to get a settlement but to no avail. So I challenged them through the legal system of which they forced me to back off through the church system by promising a settlement if I backed off.

Since I was trained up in that church system, I obeyed. But settlement didn't come. At first Sara and I couldn't understand why not, but we soon realized that the size of a man's wealth played a very key role in making judgments in the religious community. We felt extremely betrayed by this system and started to study the Holy Scriptures to try to find out how that could be. What the Scriptures revealed to us shocked us to the core. And after realizing the truths and succumbing to belief in them, healing began. The truths were very sobering, as they revealed to us how corruption had penetrated a church system that we had trusted to be absolutely Scripture-based.

I have come to fearfully respect and appreciate how I needed to be put down in order to be humbled enough to surrender and submit myself to my Creator. I was just as guilty of greed as anyone and had to repent and turn away from that system and turn to God for the first time. We do not belong to any denominational church now. But we have, as a family, committed ourselves to obeying the God of heaven and Earth, and Him alone. We belong to God's church; He provides our spiritual food, and His blessings are overwhelming. But this comes with a price tag because it means committing to the laws and commandments of God, for which much criticism does come.

Going through this experience has developed a tremendous passion to share what we have learned from the truth of God's Word, especially how the Scriptures revealed to us what changes we would have to make in our lives to be healed by our Creator. As a result of this invaluable experience, I started to write about it. Thus, we feel moved and obliged to share what we have learned through this experience with all who have ears to hear, in hopes that it may deliver some hope and encouragement to others who may find themselves in similar situations, that they also might find healing in God's truth.

I do not declare myself to be a prophet or anything of that sort. I am an average wage-earning family man with a strong passion to share what we have learned from God's truth. That is what motivated me to publish *The Commandments of God*. If any good comes from it, I pray that any and all honor and glory would go to our Creator God. Cornie Banman.

Preface

What I want to achieve with *The Commandments of God* is to show God-fearing people that the traditions of men can be a tremendous curse, especially when these traditions are what sets the standards and makes up the doctrines of a church system. According to the Holy Scriptures, God's ways are about giving and man's ways about taking. This ought to explain why man's ways of giving will usually demand something in return. So as we travel through *The Commandments of God*, I hope to bring out the point that the foundation upon which most church doctrines are established are about obeying the traditions of men. Most of these traditions come from centuries back—many even centuries before the Messiah came on the scene. They are not something that just popped up within the last few generations, although some have. But the majority go back a couple millennia or so, and that's why they have such deep and almost unmovable roots. I have done a lot of research in encyclopedias and such references, which I always compare to the Scriptures, and then base any and all decisions on the Scriptures. So in *The Commandments of God*, you will find most of my references backed by Scripture and not so much by other sources. I decided to reference as little as possible from non-Scripture sources because those materials, although they may be true, are put together by man. Therefore I am not quoting any specific church doctrines but rather relating to the results of the teachings of the doctrines that are used in the traditional systems.

My family and I learned that as soon as we committed ourselves to obeying the commandments of God, we ran into issues with the church's doctrinal system, which admits that God's commandments are good and ought to be obeyed, but not all of them. The early church fathers have labeled them as *Jewish* and *burdensome* and many other wearisome descriptions that they use to justify not observing them. It is true; the Scriptures are full of stories about burdensome commandment-keeping. But I will show you, in both the Old and New Testaments, that they never refer to the commandments of God when such terms are used in Scripture—only to the commandments of men.

Therefore, we will first see how such words and phrases are used in the Scriptures, from which I'll show how we become enslaved by keeping man's commandments. We'll look at the true scriptural meaning of liberty and that it can be obtained only by keeping God's commandments. I'll use Strong's concordance and the Hebrew and Greek Scriptures to confirm the usage of some of these words in hopes that it will help you to understand the real definitions of those terms. Then we'll look at examples from the Old and New Testaments to prove that point. We will see that there are absolutely no contradictions between the Old and New Testaments and that any and all doctrines of which the New Testament apostles have written are in perfect harmony with everything that God has ever commanded in the Old Testament. Thus we will see, by the Messiah's examples, that the traditional church doctrines are not founded upon the laws and commandments of the eternal God of Heaven and Earth.

Please read and study *The Commandments of God* with an open mind and look these Scriptures up. It is very important that you do not take this kind of information just from me, or any man for that matter, but that you prove all things from God's Scriptures. That's why I do not reference the matter of this book to any specific church doctrines. But instead, if you follow any church doctrines, I challenge you to compare them with the Word of God for your benefit.

I ask that you read this entire document before judging it. My intention is not to antagonize or condemn any person, group of people, church group, community, or society. But I do abhorrently reject and rebuke with all possible force given me the "law-done-away" doctrines with which Satan has deceived and enslaved us for many centuries, thus deceiving billions of people with that one single lie. I must warn you that I will be blunt and to the point throughout this book because I do not believe in "watering down" God's truths but prefer that they might strike us where they ought to. And I say this from my own experience; I am a testimony to this statement.

Satan deceived Eve and convinced her that God was not a good government. He tempted Eve into believing that God's ways were not good for her, that His laws and commands were restrictive, and that by not accepting His laws, but rather heeding Satan's lie, she would become all-knowing and immortal:

> But of the fruit of the tree which is in the midst of the garden, God hath said, Ye shall not eat of it, neither shall ye touch it, lest ye die. And the serpent said unto the woman, **Ye shall not surely die**: For God doth know that in the day ye eat thereof, then your eyes shall be opened, and ye shall be as gods, knowing good and evil (Gen. 3:3–5).

In like manner, Eve deceived Adam with that serpent's advice. That serpent, called Satan or the Devil (Rev. 12:9; 20:2), still uses the same approach to deceive us with the same lie: God's laws are burdens; they are for the Jews; we are not enslaved to any rules or laws; we are free from the bondage of the laws; and on he goes. And as carnal-minded, proud human beings, just like our parents of old, Adam and Eve, we still believe that same lie because, to our traditional Christian society, lawlessness has come to mean freedom. This is one of Satan's biggest and most believed lies.

Most of the New Testament was originally written in Greek and translated to other languages many centuries later. The King James Version was translated between 1604 and 1611. The Old Testament was originally written in Hebrew. I have an interlinear Hebrew-Greek-English Bible, where every word in Hebrew and Greek is numbered for the purpose of looking it up in a concordance and dictionary. I have studied the contents of the articles in this document and have included a few of the main definitions in section 1 for your information, in hopes that it will help to understand the topic of this book.

Throughout this book, you will see endnote numbers like <nomos>,[6] which indicate that you will find the Hebrew or Greek definition for that word in section 17. I have emphasized texts in Scripture verses throughout this book. All Scripture quotes are *italicized.* Nonitalicized words and phrases added among Scripture in [brackets] are also my emphasis. Quotes are as they appear in the Scripture, with the exception of the words or phrases that I have **bolded** or otherwise emphasized. This is done for clarification purposes only, so that you can see what I am emphasizing at the time. No words or phrases have been altered to any extent beyond what I've mentioned. All Scripture verses are quoted from the King James Version, unless otherwise stated.

In section 16 you will find an index of Scripture references listed in alphabetical order. You'll see a column indicating where that particular Scripture is quoted, and another column indicating where that Scripture is referenced in the book.

1. Hebrew/Greek/English Definitions for Yoke and Bondage

Isaiah 10:27: *And it shall come to pass in that day, that his **burden** shall be taken away from off thy shoulder, and his **yoke** from off thy neck, and the **yoke** shall be destroyed because of the anointing.* Hebrew for **burden**: 5448. lbo cobel, so'-bel; a load (figuratively):-burden. Hebrew for **yoke**: 5923. le `ol, ole; a yoke (as imposed on the neck), literally or figuratively:-yoke.

Jeremiah 27:8: *The nation and kingdom which will not serve the same Nebuchadnezzar the king of **Babylon**, and that will not put their neck under the **yoke** of the king of **Babylon**, that nation will I punish . . .* Hebrew for **Babylon**: 894. lbb Babel, baw-bel'; confusion; Babel (i.e., Babylon), including Babylonia and the Babylonian empire:-Babel, Babylon. Hebrew for **yoke**: 5923. le `ol, ole; (above).

Matthew 11:29-30: *Take my **yoke** upon you, and learn of me; for I am meek and lowly in heart: and ye shall find rest unto your souls. For my **yoke** is easy, and my burden is light.* Greek for **yoke**: 2218. zugos, dzoo-gos'; (to join, especially by a "yoke"); a coupling (i.e., (figuratively) servitude (a law or obligation)); also (literally) the beam of the balance (as connecting the scales)-pair of balances, yoke. Greek for

burden: 5413. phortion, for-tee'-on; an invoice (as part of freight), i.e. (figuratively) a task or service:-burden.

Acts 15:10: *Now therefore why tempt ye God, to put a* **yoke** *upon the neck of the disciples, which neither our fathers nor we were able to bear?* Greek for **yoke**: 2218. zugos, dzoo-gos'; (above).

We can see that the use of *yoke* #2218 (zugos) in Scripture refers to a coupling, a beam to balance (or equalize) the scale or load; a commitment to one's part of the terms and conditions of a contract, or covenant.

Exodus 1:14: *And they made their lives bitter with hard* **bondage**, *in mortar, and in brick, and in all manner . . .* Hebrew for **bondage**: 5656. hdbe `abodah, ab-o-daw'; work of any kind:-act, bondage, + bondservant, effect, labour, ministering(-try), office, service(-ile,-itude), tillage, use, work, X wrought.

Exodus 13:3: *Remember this day, in which ye came out from Egypt, out of the house of* **bondage**; *for by strength of hand the LORD brought you out from this place . . .* Hebrew for **bondage**: 5650. dbe `ebed, eh'-bed; a servant:-X bondage, bondman, (bond-)servant, (man-)servant.

Nehemiah 5:5: *We bring into* **bondage** *our sons and our daughters to be servants, and some of our daughters are brought unto* **bondage** *already . . .* Hebrew for **bondage**: 3533. vbk kabash, kaw-bash'; a primitive root; to tread down; hence, negatively, to disregard; positively, to conquer, subjugate, violate:-bring into bondage, force, keep under, subdue, bring into subjection.

Acts 7:6: *And God spake on this wise, That his seed should sojourn in a strange land; and that they should bring them into* **bondage**, *and entreat them evil four hundred years.* Greek for **bondage**: 1402. douloo, doo-lo'-o; to enslave (literally or figuratively):-bring into (be under) bondage, X given, become (make) servant.

2 Corinthians 11:20: *For ye suffer, if a man bring you into **bondage**, if a man devour you, if a man take of you, if a man exalt himself, if a man smite you on the face.* Greek for **bondage**: 2615. katadouloo, kat-ad-oo-lo'-o; to enslave utterly:-bring into bondage.

Galatians 4:3: *Even so we, when we were children, were in **bondage** under the **elements** of the world.* Greek for **bondage**: 1402. douloo, doo-lo'-o; (above). Greek for **elements**: 4747. stoicheion, stoy-khi'-on; something orderly in arrangement, i.e. (by implication) a serial (basal, fundamental, initial) constituent (literally), proposition (figuratively)):-element, principle, rudiment.

2 Peter 2:19: *While they promise them liberty, they themselves are the servants of corruption: for of whom a man is overcome, of the same is he brought in **bondage**.* Greek for **bondage**: 1402. douloo, doo-lo'-o; (above).

Galatians 5:1: *Stand fast therefore in the liberty wherewith Christ hath made us free, and be not **entangled** again with the **yoke** of **bondage**.* Greek for liberty: 1657. eleutheria, el-yoo-ther-ee'-ah; freedom (legitimate or licentious, chiefly moral or ceremonial):-liberty. Greek for **entangled**: 1758. enecho, en-ekh'-o; to hold in or upon (i.e., ensnare); by implication, to keep a grudge:-entangle with, have a quarrel against, urge. Greek for **yoke**: 2218. zugos, dzoo-gos'; (above). Greek for **bondage**: 1397. douleia, doo-li'-ah; slavery (ceremonially or figuratively):-bondage.

We can see that *bondage* is used in all the definitions in Scripture as a form of slavery: *slavery* #1397, "to enslave utterly" #2615, and so forth.

2. The Ten Commandments

I'm assuming that you are somewhat familiar with the Ten Commandments that God gave to mankind. They are the moral code that our Creator expects us to live by if we want to be called His children. I will briefly summarize them before we delve into the main topic of this book.

If you study them, you will see that the first stone tablet, which contains the first four commandments, is designed in a way that will train our heart and mind to worship the right God and put Him first in everything we do. Commandments five to ten on the second tablet are like the first four in that they are His instructions for us to always put others first or, at the very least, even with ourselves. This is how the Messiah summed them up:

> *Jesus said unto him, Thou shalt **love** the Lord thy God with all thy heart, and with all thy soul, and with all thy mind. This is the first and great commandment* [the first tablet]. *And the second is like unto it, Thou shalt **love** thy neighbour as thyself* [the second tablet]. *On these two commandments hang all the law and the prophets* (Matt. 22:37–40).

If we love Him and if we desire to attain eternal life, we will keep them: *If ye love me, keep my commandments* (John 14:15). *If thou wilt enter into life, keep the commandments* (Matt. 19:17).

Life is promised for keeping them; death is promised for not keeping them:

> *Behold, I set before you this day a blessing and a curse; A blessing, if ye obey the commandments of the LORD your God, which I command you this day: And a curse, if ye will not obey the commandments of the LORD your God...* (Deut. 11:26-28). *See, I have set before thee this day life and good, and death and evil; In that I command thee this day to love the LORD thy God, to walk in his ways, and to keep **his commandments** and his statutes and his judgments, that thou mayest live and multiply: and the LORD thy God shall bless thee in the land whither thou goest to possess it. But if thine heart turn away, so that thou wilt not hear, but shalt be drawn away, and worship other gods, and serve them; I denounce unto you this day, that ye shall surely perish, and that ye shall not prolong your days upon the land, whither thou passest over Jordan to go to possess it. I call heaven and earth to record this day against you, that I have set before you life and death, blessing and cursing: therefore choose life, that both thou and thy seed may live: That thou mayest love the LORD thy God, and that thou mayest obey his voice, and that thou mayest cleave unto him: for he is thy life, and the length of thy days: that thou mayest dwell in the land which the LORD sware unto*

> *thy fathers, to Abraham, to Isaac, and to Jacob,*
> *to give them* (Deut. 30:15–20).

Obedience to the Ten Commandments is how God's love for mankind is defined. That is the only recipe there is to combat selfishness and pride. Throughout the Scriptures, we find that His love and mercy for mankind is endless and way beyond what our carnal mind is able to understand. And obedience to His commandments is the only way by which mankind can attain that kind of love, which He wants us to have. The entire Torah teaching and instructions dwell wholly on the theme of developing a character of *love* and *mercy* for mankind, without which we have no forgiveness:

> *And as ye would that men should do to you,*
> *do ye also to them likewise* (Luke 6:31). *Be*
> *ye therefore merciful, as your Father also*
> *is merciful* (Luke 6:36). *And forgive us our*
> *debts, as we forgive our debtors* (Matt. 6:12).
> *For if ye forgive men their trespasses, your*
> *heavenly Father will also forgive you. But if*
> *ye forgive not men their trespasses, neither*
> *will your Father forgive your trespasses*
> (Matt. 6:14-15; read also 1 John 1:9). *Blessed*
> *are the merciful: for they shall obtain mercy*
> (Matt. 5:7).

The measure of love and mercy we have for others, is the measure of love and mercy God will have on us.

I will list the Ten Commandments and follow up with a brief summary of them, as they apply to us today.

Exodus 20:1–17:

> *1 And God spake all these words, saying,*

Tablet 1: Love toward God

First Commandment: 2 I am the LORD thy God, which have brought thee out of the land of Egypt, out of the house of bondage. 3 Thou shalt have no other gods before me. Second Commandment: 4 Thou shalt not make unto thee any graven image, or any likeness of any thing that is in heaven above, or that is in the earth beneath, or that is in the water under the earth. 5 Thou shalt not bow down thyself to them, nor serve them: for I the LORD thy God am a jealous God, visiting the iniquity of the fathers upon the children unto the third and fourth generation of them that hate me; 6 And shewing mercy unto thousands of them that love me, and keep my commandments. Third Commandment: 7 Thou shalt not take the name of the LORD thy God in vain; for the LORD will not hold him guiltless that taketh his name in vain. Fourth Commandment: 8 Remember the sabbath day, to keep it holy. 9 Six days shalt thou labour, and do all thy work: 10 But the seventh day is the sabbath of the LORD thy God: in it thou shalt not do any work, thou, nor thy son, nor thy daughter, thy manservant, nor thy maidservant, nor thy cattle, nor thy stranger that is within thy gates: 11 For in six days the LORD made heaven and earth, the sea, and all that in them is, and rested the seventh day: wherefore the LORD blessed the Sabbath day, and hallowed it.

Tablet 2: Love toward Others

Fifth Commandment: 12 Honour thy father and thy mother: that thy days may be long upon the land which the LORD thy God giveth thee. Sixth Commandment: 13 Thou shalt not kill. Seventh Commandment: 14 Thou shalt not commit adultery.

Eighth Commandment: 15 Thou shalt not steal.
Ninth Commandment: 16 Thou shalt not bear false witness against thy neighbour.
Tenth Commandment: 17 Thou shalt not covet thy neighbour's house, thou shalt not covet thy neighbour's wife, nor his manservant, nor his maidservant, nor his ox, nor his ass, nor any thing that is thy neighbour's.

In the first commandment, God clearly identifies Himself as the God who redeemed the people from the Egyptian bondage and slavery. In literal modern-day terms, it means that He is the God who redeemed us from the bondage to sin and death. Egypt is in a type of sin in scriptural terms in that they worshipped gods made by hand, and because of the hard slavery that they brutally forced upon the Hebrew people which greatly oppressed them (Exod. 1). Thus, the Hebrew people were in Egyptian bondage. They were descendants of Abraham and called the children of Israel. The Exodus story is an extremely colorful account about how the God of Abraham, of Isaac, and of Jacob redeemed the Hebrew people from that bondage. God solemnly declares in the first commandment that He is the One who delivered them from that bondage, wherefore He says "worship me, and none other." In the same way, He is the same God who redeemed us from the bondage to sin and death, by dying on the tree to pay for the penalty of our sins.

In the second commandment, He defines Himself as a jealous God, wherefore we are to worship no other God but Him. He does not like it when other gods get the glory which belongs to Him. He promises blessings to thousands of generations for those who keep His commandments, and curses for three to four generations for breaking them. Please realize the seriousness of this commandment. He's talking to you and me about our children!

I will put this as plainly as I can because we need to understand how this commandment applies directly to our everyday life, to our children, to their children, and so on. I'll spend some extra time to explain the far-reaching implications of this particular commandment. And I'll follow up with an example from the Exodus journey.

God is literally telling you and me that, if we refuse to keep His commandments, practice all ten of them, the next three to four generations will be cursed. It's just that plain. Let's put this into proper perspective. This literally means that our children, our grandchildren, our great-grandchildren, and potentially our great-great-grandchildren will be cursed for our not keeping the commandments of our Creator and for using some other instructions than His for the health, welfare, and success of us and our family. But, if we diligently practice His commandments, He will bless thousands of generations to follow. Can you see how great, excellent, and far-reaching His love is for us if we obey His Commandments? I know, it is way over our heads to comprehend how God contrasts between love and hate. But I don't think that He could have expressed the magnitude of His love any clearer.

Let's think for a moment about how God's love is defined. His love in the scriptural text is the Greek word #26 <agape>.[1] It is a charitable love that the carnal mind cannot fully understand. The word comes from the base of word #25 <agapao>, [1a] which is the type of love that we're more familiar with, as a social love. If we chase it down, it eventually ends up as the word #5384 <philos>, [1b] which denotes a fond friend. I hope you get the idea. When you come across the word *friend* in the King James Version, it is translated from the word *philos.* So we can see that godly love is a charitable love of a very high degree, which can only come from the extreme depth within the main root system, which is our Creator, the God of Israel.

Knowing this, we can see that the love that God impresses upon us through the second commandment stands out tremendously and is easily overlooked. Let me explain what I mean by this, because this is very important to understand how God's love is involved even when He punishes us. When we look at His blessings for obeying His commandments, He applies them to thousands of generations. But when He promises His curses for disobedience to His commandments, He applies them to only a few generations. Please don't misunderstand me here. I don't mean by this that a few generations of curses aren't significant, because they are very significant, almost unthinkable. But what I'm trying to convey is the contrast between the curses and blessings in light of His love for His creation. He curses a few generations in hopes of correcting them, thus bringing them back to Him again. I hope you can understand this. And if you can't, please study it in the Scriptures until you can.

If you want to learn more about these particular blessings and curses, they are described very intensely in Leviticus 26 and Deuteronomy 28. I urge you to study them to get a grasp of the vastness of His promises and of the blessings and curses. And if you continue to diligently study the whole book of Deuteronomy, you will see that those prophecies are still valid today and that all scriptural prophecies thereafter are based on what Moses already prophesied there, about 3,500 years ago, just before the Israelites crossed the Jordan River:

> *When thou art in tribulation, and all these things are come upon thee, **even in the latter days**, if thou turn to the LORD thy God, and shalt be obedient unto his voice. (For the LORD thy God is a **merciful** God;) **he will not forsake thee**, neither destroy thee, nor forget the covenant of thy fathers which he sware unto them* (Deut. 4:30–31).

In case you're not familiar with these Scriptures, I will give you a brief chronology of the relevant ones, with hopes that it will help you to understand the depth of these blessings and curses. I will give the Scripture references so you can look them up and read not just the quoted verses but read around them to get the feel for the storyline. It is very important that we understand the roots and the far-reaching implications of these prophecies to be able to understand the Scriptures as a whole and their purpose as they apply to us today, tomorrow, and thereafter.

The first five books (the Torah) are referred to as the books of Moses because God had Moses write them. These books are Genesis, Exodus, Leviticus, Numbers, and Deuteronomy.

The book of Genesis is often referred to as the book of beginnings, which it truly is. Everything that has happened in the past, everything that you see happening today, and everything that is yet to come has its prophecy rooted in the book of Genesis. From the time of Adam and Eve up to the great flood, the Scriptures reveal only limited information. But there is enough to suffice us for what we need to know about how sovereign a God He is, that He is the only God who has true control of the universe as we know it, and that He has always hated sin. He gave us sufficient evidence to show that His laws and commandments were "from the beginning." This has an important bearing on the controversy that we face today with a class of people who claim that God's commandments started at Mount Sinai, with the implication that God commanded only the Jewish people to keep them. The rest of *The Commandments of God*, after this section, will address exactly that controversial topic.

But while we're on this topic, I will present one argument to consider, maybe as a kick-off to the remaining sections of *The Commandments of God*. Adam was created about 2,500 years before God wrote the Ten Commandments into stone tablets on Mount Sinai. Scripture clearly states what sin is: *Sin is the transgression of the law* (1 John 3:4). As we saw in the preface, Adam and Eve sinned (Gen. 3:3–5). Satan had already sinned wherefore he lost his rights to God's kingdom, which had to have occurred before Adam and Eve sinned. Cain sinned by murdering Abel (Gen. 4:8). Finally, God flooded the whole world for its continual sinning (Gen. 6:5) and saved only righteous Noah with his family (Gen. 7:1). Only a few generations after the flood, Noah's great-grandson Nimrod built cities and the Tower of Babel (Gen. 10:10), which God abhorred, wherefore He confounded the language (Gen. 11:7). *Babel* #0894 <babel>² in Hebrew means *confusion*. Thereafter, when you read about Babylon (as a system or nation), or Chaldean (as a people), it relates directly to the attributes of that account, which depicts Nimrod as a type of Satan. A short while later, the cities of Sodom and Gomorrah, together with all except three people, were destroyed by fire from God (Gen. 19:24–25) for sodomy and fornication, which are sins (Gen. 13:13; 18:20; also read 2 Peter 2:6; Jude 7; Rev 11:8). If God had no laws and commandments at that time, how could they have sinned? It says that Noah was righteous, what was it measured against? ***All thy commandments are righteousness*** (Ps. 119:172). So we know that God's commandments have been "from the beginning" (1 John 2:7).

After Satan deceived Eve, God promised that He would bring a child into this world who would destroy Satan and eventually remove him from the face of this earth. This promised child is mentioned in Genesis 3:15 and would be delivered through the covenant that He made with faithful Abraham in Genesis 12–18. That covenant was later transferred to Abraham's son Isaac in Genesis 26:3–4. Through this covenant, God would bless all nations (Gen. 12:3; 17:4; 26:4). In other words, everyone who follows the faith of Abraham and keeps God's commandments as he had would be blessed: *Because that Abraham obeyed my voice, and kept my charge,* **my commandments,** *my statutes, and my laws* (Gen. 26:5). Then in Genesis 32 and 35, that covenant was transferred to Isaac's son Jacob, whose name God changed to Israel at that point. From there forward, to the present and future, God referred to His people as Israelites; the Israel of God (Gal. 6:16).

In Exodus 1–2, the children of Israel are enslaved in Egyptian bondage. Chapters 3–13 hold the account of God using Moses to deliver Abraham's descendants, the children of Israel, out of Egyptian bondage and slavery. By bringing them out, God exercises great miracles and extreme judgments in order to prove His great power and His sovereignty to the world. In chapter 12, God ordains the LORD's Passover, which shows vividly how the observance of it saved the lives of the people who observed it, and killed the firstborn in the households of those who didn't observe it (Heb. 11:28; Luke 22; 1 Cor. 11:22-27). In Exodus 12:38, we read that there were many Gentiles included in this Passover service and the journey out of Egypt. Chapter 14 describes the Israelites' miraculous Red Sea crossing and the drowning of the Egyptian army that pursued them (Heb. 11:29). In Exodus 16, God reestablishes the proper timing and observance of the fourth commandment, regarding the LORD's seventh-day Sabbath, by supplying quail and manna for food for six days and a double portion on the sixth day to suffice them for the LORD's seventh day Sabbath. Chapters 17–20 take us to Mount Sinai, from where God personally speaks the Ten Commandments to the people and writes them onto two tables of stone with His own finger. Chapters 21–24 contain the civil laws for their civil conduct as a nation on this earth. In chapter 24, the covenant is made as a binding agreement between God and His people and is ratified with blood.

This covenant is a contract in which God basically says, "If you will abide by my rules, these are the blessings that

I promise. If you don't abide by the rules of this contract, here are the curses that I promise." God plays fair; He is just and keeps His promises. These blessings and curses are described in Leviticus 26 and Deuteronomy 28. In Exodus 25–30 God gives instructions to Moses on how to build the tabernacle with the ark of the covenant with the mercy seat in the Holy Place, and all the furniture for it; which depicts our heart as His temple and tabernacle (dwelling) today. In chapters 29–30, God ordains and consecrates Aaron as the head of the Levitical priesthood and his sons as priests for the congregation. In chapter 31, God establishes a special perpetual Sabbath covenant which will identify His people. Chapter 32 is where they build the golden calf while Moses is up on the mountain getting more instructions from God. From this point on, the instructions for the sacrificial and ritualistic ordinances and ceremonies and laws continue to be added and explained as they journey through the wilderness.

The book of Leviticus continues the prescription and ordination of the Levitical priesthood, judgments, statutes, and laws for the governance of His people as a Holy nation. It describes the sacrifices, sin offerings, and its ordinances in great and full detail. Chapters 3, 17, and 19 forbid the eating of fat and blood. In chapter 8, Aaron and his sons are consecrated as priests. Chapter 11 covers God's food laws; He tells us which beasts He created for food and which ones not. Chapters 12–15 cover health issues and purification. Chapters 18–21 cover a variety of laws regarding marriage, lust, immorality, adultery, incest, sodomy, whoredom, passing seed to Moloch, observing times, wizardry, and witchcraft. Chapter 23 lays out the feasts of the LORD, also called God's Holy days, in which the seventh-day Sabbath is included. Chapter 25 covers the land Sabbath and the year of Jubilee. Chapter 26 vividly describes God's promised blessings for obedience to His commandments and curses for disobedience to His commandments. Chapter 27 has financial instructions and tithing rules. Each and every law that we find in this book was designed by God in such a way that it would train a habit of obedience into the hearts and minds of His children, so that they would learn to obey His moral and spiritual laws, the Ten Commandments, from their hearts. God calls this habit of obedience the circumcision of the heart. Each and every one of these laws is designed by God to improve the quality and quantity of life and health for mankind. God specifically designed each of these laws to be used as the ultimate maintenance guide for His excellent creation. The result would be that we could then love God from our heart, likewise love our neighbor, and show mercy to mankind.

The book of Numbers is a diary and journal of records pertaining to the Israelites' forty-year wilderness journey to Canaan.

The book of Deuteronomy has important information for us today and for our future. When the Israelites reached the Jordan River, Moses summarized everything he had taught the generation of Israelites he led out of Egypt, and passed it on to that current generation. God's laws, commandments, judgments, and statutes were rehearsed and delivered to that new generation. He reminded them of their stiffneckedness, and their rebellious and uncircumcised hearts, wherefore the whole generation of people who had seen Egypt, except Joshua and Caleb, were not allowed to cross that river into Canaan, the land of milk and honey. Only the new generation (little ones) age nineteen and under (Num. 14) were allowed to enter. The previous generations had not diligently kept God's Commandments, wherefore they perished in the wilderness (also Heb. 3:7–11). This is a promised curse for forsaking God's commandments (Lev 26; Deut 28). So Moses gave this new generation a crash course of all that had occurred up to that time. Notice that Moses gives them many strong prophetic warnings about how the foreign gods on the other side of the river would entice them to get them to flirt with them in order to steer them away from the God of Abraham. He tells them that he won't be crossing that river and that Joshua and Caleb would lead them from there on. Joshua and Caleb get ordained and blessed, and they replace Moses. And they took the children of Israel across the Jordan River. God took Moses up to the mountain, showed him the promised land, took the breath out of him, and personally buried him, where he still is (Heb. 11).

The third commandment forbids us to use the LORD's name in vain. This has much-farther-reaching implications than merely using His name as slang. A much weightier aspect of it is when His name or authority is used to snare people into a religious system. The Messiah testified that false prophets would deceive people with His name; using His name as bait: *And Jesus answered and said unto them, Take heed that no man deceive you. For many shall come in my name, saying, **I am Christ**; and shall deceive many* (Matt. 24:4–5). He is saying that people will say that He, the Lord, is the Messiah, to trick us into believing that they are preaching the true Messiah, while actually preaching another messiah.

The fourth commandment points us to the LORD's Sabbath day of rest. God created the universe, trees, herbs, man, beasts, and all things which are in it in six days (Gen. 1:1–2:1). Then on the seventh day, He rested from His great work and hallowed and sanctified it as a day of rest: *And God blessed the seventh day, and sanctified <qadash>*[3] *it: because that in it he had rested from all his work which God created and made* (Gen. 2:3; see also Heb. 4). *Sanctified* means *consecrated, set apart for God's holy purpose.* He commands for it to be observed on the seventh day of the week. The keeping of it on its proper day will testify to the world that we serve the God who created heaven and earth and all things in it. An easily forgotten aspect of this commandment is that it commands us to work the other six days: *Six days shalt thou labour* (Exod. 20:9). And the Scriptures have plenty of testimony to this. People like Noah, Moses, and all the prophets of old labored for God until the very day He took away their breath. And likewise did all the apostles. None of them retired at a certain predetermined age. They worked six days and worshipped on the Lord's Sabbath until their last breath.

These first four commandments, which the Messiah called great, are the main and fundamental commandments that are to be kept at all cost, not even sparing life itself, for His name's sake. But this does not take away from the importance of the remaining six commandments from the second tablet. Commandments five to ten pertain to our relationship with our father and mother, our brethren, and our neighbor; and if we fail at any of them, we cannot have a relationship with our heavenly Father. This is how John put it: *If a man say, I love God, and hateth his brother, he is a liar: for he that loveth not his brother whom he hath seen, how can he love God whom he hath not seen? And this commandment have we from him, That he who loveth God love his brother also* (1 John 4:20–21). In 1 John 3:15, he explains why: *Whosoever hateth his brother is a murderer: and ye know that no murderer hath eternal life abiding in him.* John cites this from what the Messiah said in the Sermon on the Mount, in which He explains the spiritual aspects of a few of God's commandments:

> *Ye have heard that it was said by them of old time, Thou shalt not kill; and whosoever shall kill shall be in danger of the judgment: But I say unto you, That whosoever is angry with his brother without a cause shall be in danger of the judgment: and whosoever shall say to his brother, Raca, shall be in danger of the council: but whosoever shall say, Thou fool, shall be in danger of hell fire ... Ye have heard*

> *that it was said by them of old time, Thou shalt not commit adultery: But I say unto you, That whosoever looketh on a woman to lust after her hath committed adultery with her already in his heart* (Matt. 5:21–22, 27–28).

God sees our heart. If our heart is circumcised, that's how God measures us, as the Messiah put it in the Sermon on the Mount. In the days of old, you were stoned for doing physical labor on the Lord's Sabbath day. Now, if we plug in the same spiritual aspect as He did for the murder and adultery commandments, we would be guilty of death for merely thinking about work or finances on His Sabbath day.

The circumcision of one's heart is loving from our heart, and it's not something new. The Messiah cited what He had Moses train to the Israelites 3,500 years ago (Lev. 19:17–18). The Messiah explained the spiritual aspect of the Ten Commandments. That is to say, if we as much as not love our brother, we have committed murder in our heart, wherefore eternal life cannot be in us. To gain eternal life, we must sacrifice our self-life for our brethren. This means that we must be prepared to willingly give up everything for our brethren, if need be. And that is what our Messiah did for you and me: *Hereby perceive we **the love of God**, because **he laid down his life for us**: and we ought to lay down our lives for the brethren* (1 John 3:16). That is how John explains the love of God, which we must have in our heart to enter into life. The Messiah said that to have eternal life required keeping the commandments (Matt. 19:17). Simply put, if I deny any one of the Ten Commandments, even one jot or tittle, it is impossible to have true love for God. That's exactly how James penciled it: *For whosoever shall keep the whole law, and yet offend in one point, he is guilty of all* (James 2:10).

Commandments five through ten all bear on the principle of love and mercy for the neighbor, summed up as *love your neighbor as yourself* (Lev 19:18; Mat 22:39). That's also how Paul described it:

> *Owe no man any thing, but to love one another: for he that loveth another hath fulfilled the law. For this, Thou shalt not commit adultery, Thou shalt not kill, Thou shalt not steal, Thou shalt not bear false witness, Thou shalt not covet; and if there be any other commandment, it is briefly comprehended in this saying, namely, Thou shalt love thy neighbour as thyself. Love worketh no ill to his neighbour: therefore love is the fulfilling of the law* (Rom. 13:8–10).

I hope this helps to understand that obedience to the Ten Commandments is essential to produce love for God and the neighbor.

3. The Protestant System

I occasionally use the terms *traditional church system*, *traditional Christian[s]*, and *Protestant system*. I will try to explain what I mean by these terms.

There are many different church denominations in this world where a preacher will meet with his congregation, typically on Sunday morning, a time they have chosen to rest and worship their [G]god. Some have their worship assemblies on other days of the week. All of them have chosen a specific day for religious reasons. Most of these will also gather and worship on days such as New Year's, Easter, and Christmas. Celebrating these holidays and worshipping on Sunday morning is a system that did not start with but was adopted by the Roman Catholic system in about 317–327 AD. That's when the Roman Emperor, Constantine I the Great, adopted the churches and any and all religious groups of his whole kingdom as one universal church system and called it Christianity, which was later named the *Holy Roman Catholic Church*. The word *Catholic* means *universal*. As we can see, the foundation of that system consists of doctrines from a horde of different religions and beliefs.

Throughout the centuries, many groups lost faith in that system, wherefore they broke away and formed their own denominational churches. These churches are called

Protestant churches (protesting Catholics), a term that applies to all churches that can trace their ancestry back to the Catholic system.

The definition for *Protestant* on the online *Encarta World English Dictionary* (North American Edition):

> *Member of church rejecting papal authority: a member or adherent of any denomination of the Western Christian church that rejects papal authority and some fundamental Roman Catholic doctrines, and believes in justification by faith. The formulation of Protestants' beliefs began with the Reformation in the 16th century.*

(Similar aspects might also apply to other religious groups, but my focus in this book will be on the protestant system, in which I was raised and baptized).

These groups separated from that Romanized system in order to break free from certain nonscriptural doctrines, with full intentions to go back to using only the Holy Scripture as their church doctrines. But the church fathers did not let go of many of the pagan traditions with which they had become so familiar and entangled. Maybe they enjoyed them too much, especially the commercial aspect of some of those doctrines. But now they are enjoying those accepted traditional doctrines without the Catholic pope. Most of today's traditional church denominations are descendants of that system in one form or another. Most of the traditional doctrines are established upon a belief that the laws and commandments of God were nailed to the tree together with the Messiah because the keeping of them was supposedly too burdensome and grievous a task, wherefore we are now saved by grace alone, without obedience to His commandments. So they preach that to be the very liberty with which the Messiah has set us free, wherewith they explain away the need to keep them.

Therefore, when the controlling people from this system read any words or phrases in the Scriptures that suggest hard and grievous burdens, they immediately jump to the conclusion that those terms are referring to the results or the consequences of obeying God's laws and commandments. They conclude that these laws were passed on to only the Jews of the Old Testament and as such are forbidden to be used in the New Testament church. These are very misleading and dangerous doctrines because they imply that God took the children of Israel out of the Egyptian bondage and slavery only to put them into His legal bondage and slavery. This doctrine makes our loving heavenly Father and Creator out to be a cruel, unjust, oppressive, tyrannical, and dictating god. As we will see, this cannot be! Let's check it out in the Scriptures.

When the Scriptures talk about burdens, something grievous and hard to be borne, weak and beggarly elements of this world, yoke of bondage, and so on, we will see that those definitions do not describe the result of being obedient to God's laws but rather that it defines the result of being enslaved to the bondage of man's laws by which we forsake the liberty of God's laws. The Lord makes that very point distinctively clear: *Come unto me, all ye that labour and are heavy laden, and I will give you rest. Take my yoke upon you, and learn of me; for I am meek and lowly in heart: and ye shall find rest unto your souls. For my yoke is easy, and my burden is light* (Matt. 11:28–30). The burden God places on us is light because of His great love for us. As we learned earlier in section 2, I'm sure that we all agree that the love in the Scriptures, God's <agape>[1] love, is something that we cannot understand to the full, because as the apostle Paul says, our carnal mind is hatred against God and not obedient to His laws. And mankind will struggle with carnality as long as we live. Just as Paul said that he was yet carnal years after his conversion, so are we: *For we know that the law is spiritual: but I am carnal, sold under sin* (Rom. 7:14). *Because the carnal mind is **enmity** <echthra>*[4] *against God: for it is not **subject** <hupotasso>*[5] *to the law of God, neither indeed can be* (Rom. 8:7). We will learn how the words in the Scriptures refer to the kind of love that the Messiah demonstrated for us on the tree of Calvary and how He wants us to achieve that same kind of love. My hope is that by the time we get to the end of *The Commandments of God*, we will understand how to attain this kind of love, where we can find it, and where we won't find it. I will now start with an important instruction as to how we ought to study Scripture.

4. Unambiguous Scriptures in the Old and New Testaments

When studying any topic in the Holy Scriptures, the first important step is to get acquainted with the unambiguous Scriptures. The simple and unmistakable Scriptures is what *The Commandments of God* is based upon, with the help of God the Father, through faith in the precious blood of the His Son's sacrifice, who is the author, finisher, and revealer of His Holy Scriptures. And that same author promised that His Scriptures will not contradict: *The scripture cannot be broken* (John 10:35).

Only the eternal God can give us the wisdom and knowledge required to understand His Word:

> *If any of you lack wisdom, let him ask of God, that giveth to all men liberally, and upbraideth not; and it shall be given him. But let him ask in faith, nothing wavering* (James 1:5–6). *And whatsoever we ask, we receive of him, because we keep his commandments, and do those things that are pleasing in his sight* (1 John 3:22). We need to obey His commandments to be able to understand His Word: *The fear*

*of the LORD is the beginning of wisdom: a
good understanding have all they that do his
commandments: his praise endureth for ever*
(Ps. 111:10).

The surety of the Holy Scriptures: We can know with
absolute certainty that the Scriptures will always support,
reinforce, compliment, and align with each other in
absolute and total harmony, from Genesis to Revelation,
as I refer to the Scriptures whenever I reference it. We
have that wonderful promise from our Savior, wherefore
we can totally rely upon His unchanging instructions.
It is very important to let Scripture interpret Scripture:
*Knowing this first, that no prophecy of the scripture is of any
private interpretation* (2 Peter 1:20). And to bear in mind
that all Scripture is God-breathed and must be studied
accordingly:

> *Study to shew thyself approved unto God, a
> workman that needeth not to be ashamed,
> rightly dividing the word of truth* (2 Tim.
> 2:15). *And that from a child thou hast
> known the holy scriptures, which are able
> to make thee wise unto salvation through
> faith which is in Christ Jesus. All scripture is
> given by inspiration of God, and is profitable
> for doctrine, for reproof, for correction, for
> instruction in righteousness: That the man
> of God may be perfect, thoroughly furnished
> unto all good works* (2 Tim. 3:15–17).

All Scriptures come from God, who cannot lie—*which
God, that cannot lie* (Titus 1:2)—and not from any man:
*For the prophecy came not in old time by the will of man:
but holy men of God spake as they were moved by the Holy
Ghost* (2 Peter 1:21; read also Rom. 15:4). Peter specifically

refers to the prophecies of the Old Testament. And this eternal God does not change: *For I am the LORD, I change not...* (Mal. 3:6). *Jesus Christ the same yesterday, and to day, and for ever* (Heb. 13:8; read also James 1:17). This defines the Holy Scriptures, in which, if there be found just one contradiction, would be rendered useless. But the Messiah promises that it can't happen (John 10:35, quoted above). And God does not confuse His Word: *For God is not the author of confusion...* (1 Cor. 14:33). The task of confusing the Scriptures is left to the proud and religious theologians: *At that time Jesus answered and said, I thank thee, O Father, Lord of heaven and earth, because thou hast hid these things from the wise and prudent, and hast revealed them unto babes* (Matt. 11:25; read also 1 Cor. 1:19-30). God knows that the proud theologians are commandment-breakers, just like the glory-seeking scribes and Pharisees, wherefore He will not give them understanding of His Word (Ps. 111:10). They must confuse the Scripture in a way that others can't understand it without their interpretation of it. And they pervert them in a way that will tickle the listeners' ears: *For the time will come when they will not endure sound doctrine; but after their own lusts shall they heap to themselves teachers, having itching ears; And they shall turn away their ears from the truth, and shall be turned unto fables* (2 Tim. 4:3–4). This perversion helps to fill the pews, which in turn fills the offering bag. Thus, glory be to them. Their glory-seeking and control-mongering mission is accomplished.

We will review a few simple and unambiguous Scriptures from the New Testament regarding the validity and purpose of God's moral and spiritual laws, and the blessings and curses for the keeping and breaking of them. We need to get acquainted with these before we dig any deeper into this subject. Take time to read and understand these following Scriptures in order to get grounded by them, and remember the words from our Savior: no Scripture can contradict any point of another Scripture.

The following are words that the Messiah spoke anywhere from ten to thirty-five years before they were written down as Gospels. It's important to acknowledge this because, although it is written in what we refer to as the New Testament, the Messiah rehearsed it from the Old Testament, of which He actually is the unchanging author:

> *Think not that I am come to destroy the law, or the prophets: I am not come to destroy, but to fulfil. For verily I say unto you, Till heaven and earth pass, one jot or one tittle shall in no wise pass from the law, till all be fulfilled. Whosoever therefore shall break one of these least commandments, and shall teach men so, he shall be called the least in the kingdom of heaven: but whosoever shall do and teach them, the same shall be called great in the kingdom of heaven* (Matt. 5:17–19). *And it is easier for heaven and earth to pass, than one tittle of the law to fail* (Luke 16:17). *Heaven and earth shall pass away: but my words shall not pass away* (Luke 21:33). *If ye love me, keep my commandments* (John 14:15). *If thou wilt enter into life, keep the commandments* (Matt. 19:17).

The inspired words from His apostles, which were written from twenty to sixty-five years after the resurrection of the Messiah:

> *And hereby we do know that we know him, if we keep his commandments. He that saith, I know him, and keepeth not his commandments, is a liar, and the truth is*

not in him (1 John 2:3–4). *By this we know that we love the children of God, when we love God, and keep his commandments. For this is the love of God, that we keep his commandments: and his commandments are not grievous* (1 John 5:2–3). *Circumcision is nothing, and uncircumcision is nothing, but the keeping of the commandments of God* (1 Cor. 7:19). *The doers of the law shall be justified* (Rom. 2:13). *Wherefore the law is holy, and the commandment holy, and just, and good* (Rom. 7:12). *For in Jesus Christ neither circumcision availeth any thing, nor uncircumcision; but faith which worketh by love* (Gal. 5:6; see also 2 Timothy 3:15–17 quoted above). *Whosoever hateth his brother is a murderer: and ye know that no murderer hath eternal life abiding in him* (1 John 3:15). *If thou kill, thou art become a transgressor of the law* (James 2:11). *Whosoever committeth sin transgresseth also the law: for sin is the transgression of the law* (1 John 3:4). *All unrighteousness is sin . . .* (1 John 5:17). *For all thy commandments are righteousness* (Ps. 119:172). *Faith without works is dead* (James 2:20). *For this is the covenant that I will make with the house of Israel after those days, saith the Lord; I will put my laws into their mind, and write them in their hearts: and I will be to them a God, and they shall be to me a people* (Heb. 8:10). *The love of God is shed abroad in our hearts by the Holy Ghost which is given unto us* (Rom. 5:5). ***The scripture cannot be broken*** (John 10:35).

We'll look at a couple verses to see that the death penalty, the curse of the law, is still in effect. By touching the forbidden tree, Eve broke God's commandment, for which the penalty was death: *But of the tree of the knowledge of good and evil, thou shalt not eat of it: for in the day that thou eatest thereof* **thou shalt surely die** (Gen. 2:17). If we break His commandments today, the wage is still death: *For the wages of sin is* **death** . . . (Rom. 6:23).

We will study and summarize these above-mentioned Scriptures, which I call the foundational and infallible instructions of the New Testament by which we must live if and when we accept the Messiah as our personal Lord, Savior, and Redeemer from our past walk in sin (Rom. 3:25), whereby we become justified by God's grace, through our faith in the blood of the Messiah's sacrifice. At this point we have promised to follow in His footsteps wherever He takes us. And the Holy Scripture is His road map for us, which we must follow as a guide. We must ask and allow Him to guide and direct us through each and every thought of each day of our life. Please study Deuteronomy 6, where God gives instructions how to diligently train (circumcise) our hearts and minds.

Our walk with Him is the sanctification period, whereby God sets us apart for His holy purpose, for His honor and glory. And this is the part that the carnal mind hates, because it hates rules and will stop at nothing to avoid being obligated to rules, especially when they come from God. That's because obedience to God's moral laws and commandments will inevitably invite persecution from the pagan-religious society around and among us. It is amazing how the animal kingdom and the whole universe have always remained obedient and loyal to the laws of the Creator. God gave everything that He made an instinct, as we call it, preprogrammed to do what He designed it for, except for humans, whom He gave a brain to think on their own and make their own choices in life, thus giving us free moral agency to choose between right (God's ways) and wrong (man's ways; the god's of this world). And humans are the only created beings who will vehemently reject their Creator by rejecting His instructions and laws. And God did give us that right and freedom to choose (Read 1 Sam 8).

Nevertheless, when we commit ourselves to Him and decide to take His yoke upon us in order to follow Him in His ways, we enter into a new covenant (agreement, contract) with Him. We have now chosen to follow in His footsteps as He gives us His personal instructions throughout His Holy Scriptures.

In light of this, we need to realize and accept as an absolute truth that these simple and unmistakable Scriptures must, and always will, agree with all other Scriptures. We have that wonderful promise from our Savior. Therefore we can know with absolute certainty that any and all harder-to-understand Scriptures must, and always will, harmonize with the ones that are simple and easy to understand. If we come across an ambiguous Scripture, and it appears to contradict an unambiguous Scripture, we must accept the fact that we do not understand the ambiguous Scripture. In simple terms, a hard-to-understand Scripture cannot and will not contradict an easy-to-understand Scripture.

The Lord assures us that no part of God's laws will pass until heaven and Earth pass away. John says in plain words that to have God's love in us means keeping God's commandments. Paul adds that these commandments are holy, just, and good, and that we acquire the necessary faith through that love, wherefore he concludes that the doers of them shall be justified. He says that all Scripture must be used to become wise unto salvation. James says, as did our Savior, that we sin by breaking even a least point of the laws, and he adds that our works must show our faith in our beliefs and that they do, just as did Abraham's sacrifice of his only true son. All true believers in the Messiah know that we are still able to sin; and John says that sin is the transgression of the laws and that just hating another person from the heart makes one a murderer. It's vital that we keep God's commandments to be able to have His love shed abroad in our hearts, because not loving is hating. Hebrews 8 clearly states that God will put His laws into the hearts and minds of His people. In order for this to happen, there must still be laws. We can see some very important reasons why the commandments of God must still exist and that they must be kept to be able to have God's love in us, wherewith to fulfill the laws. *Love worketh no ill to his neighbour: therefore love is the fulfilling of the law* (Rom. 13:10).

Based totally and absolutely on this knowledge from our great and undividing merciful God and Father, I have, with His help, diligently studied the subject of concern and based everything upon and around the principles of these unambiguous Scriptures knowing, and bearing in mind, that no part of any Scripture will contradict another Scripture. And I trust that we will learn to accept that truth, so that we may know the truth that God wants us to learn to live by and walk with for His honor and glory, while it is at the same time to our benefit. Please allow these truths to take root and become fully grounded in you.

Through this knowledge, we will see that the teachings that the Messiah and His apostles are using to reveal God's great plans for mankind have ironically been taken almost entirely in the opposite direction by the traditional church system. There it is preached that the laws of God were done away by the same Lord who said that not one jot or tittle would pass from it. I will show you examples that all Scriptures, from Genesis to Revelation, are still valid and binding today. The page that divides the Old from the New Testament was put there by religious theologians, which should never have been done. Most of the "law-done-away" doctrines have been established after that division of God's Word and as such have caused tremendous scriptural confusion. And of course, that is an accomplishment of Satan, the Devil, and none other.

Thus it has inspired me to put onto paper what I have learned through this study, and *The Commandments of God* is the result of it. My hope and prayer is that you will not take this information just from me but that it would rather by some tiny measure provoke you to study it and prove to yourself, from the Holy Scriptures, what the truths are regarding these matters, for your own benefit. May any and all honor and glory go to God, where it is due, as He is the author, finisher, and revealer of the Holy Scriptures, which contains His great plans for us (Heb. 5:9; 12:2).

There is a common belief in traditional Christianity that the New Testament church ought not use Old Testament Scriptures in any way or form to make up church doctrines. At this time I want to show a few examples about the unity and harmony of these two books. There will not be found any doctrines or prophecies in the New Testament that don't have their roots in the Old Testament. Paul makes this plain in 2 Timothy 3:15–17 where he reminds Timothy that the knowledge that he had from the Holy Scriptures is able to make him wise unto salvation, through faith in the Messiah, and that all Scripture is God-breathed, by which the man of God may be fully furnished unto all good works. What Holy Scriptures was Paul referring to? When Paul wrote this letter Timothy already knew about faith in the Messiah; but at that time they had only the Old Testament scrolls. And he points to those Scriptures decades after the crucifixion. If the Old Testament Scriptures had become obsolete, why didn't Paul tell Timothy to dump what he had learned from his youth and only go by the New Testament Scriptures? Why not? Because Paul believed the Messiah when He said that not one jot or tittle had passed from the law and the prophets (Matt. 5:17–19), that is, the Scriptures, which he encouraged Timothy to hang on to. He said in 1 Corinthians 7:19 and Romans 2:13 and 7:12 that it is important that we keep God's commandments. What? This is the same Paul who, according to traditional Christianity, preached against keeping God's commandments in the New Testament church because it apparently involves works that cut you off from God's grace. The law-done-away preachers have labeled commandment-keeping as *works,* such as trying to earn one's salvation. The Messiah said in numerous occasions that only faithful commandment-keepers and teachers of them would enter into the kingdom of God (Matt. 5:17–19; 19:17; Rev 12:17; 14:12; 22:14). He confirms that they are still binding and that not an iota of them would pass until heaven and earth pass. If you are reading these words, earth is still with us; it's just that simple. According to the words of the Messiah not an iota of the laws has been destroyed. Some aspects of them have been fulfilled, one being the sacrifice of the Messiah as the Lamb of God. That is why we no longer sacrifice animals to atone for our sins. (We will see more of this later.)

While the Messiah taught His disciples from the Holy Scriptures, before and after the crucifixion, they had only the Old Testament scrolls, which still is God's holy, sacred, and living Word. Matthew wrote these words down about ten to fifteen years after the Messiah recited them from the Old Testament prophecies:

> *It is written, Man shall not live by bread alone, but by **every word** that proceedeth out of the mouth of God* (Matt. 4:4, quoted from Deut. 8:3). *It is written again, Thou shalt not tempt the Lord thy God* (Matt. 4:7, quoted from Deut. 6:16). *Get thee hence, Satan: for it is written, Thou shalt worship the Lord thy God,*

> *and him only shalt thou serve* (Matt. 4:10,
> quoted from Deut. 6:13).

This is the account where the Lord was tempted by Satan in the wilderness. In all three occasions, He defeats Satan with His Father's holy words from the Old Testament Scriptures. And He preached from it to the people of His time: *And he said unto them, These are the words which I spake unto you, while I was yet with you, that all things must be fulfilled, which were written in the law of Moses, and in the prophets, and in the psalms, concerning me* (Luke 24:44). The Messiah is referring to the prophecies of the Old Testament. What He had gone through just prior to the time He said this, the crucifixion and resurrection, is a part of the fulfillment of which He spoke. And as you're reading this, the prophecies of those very same Scriptures are being yet further fulfilled. The fulfillment of these prophecies will not be completed until He returns again to rule for a thousand years with Satan locked away (Rev. 20:2–4). This will occur after the great tribulation, which is the first resurrection. And after the thousand years, there is another resurrection, the great white throne judgment (Rev. 20). We will not go into details on this topic, because it deserves a book of its own. I am showing this only to prove that there is much more, wonderful and terrible events, yet to be fulfilled.

The Messiah preached about how we are to worship God and how to love Him and others, by quoting directly from the old covenant in the Old Testament Scriptures:

> *Master, which is the great commandment in the law? Jesus said unto him, Thou shalt* **love the Lord thy God** *with all thy heart, and with all thy soul, and with all thy mind. This is the first and great commandment. And the second is like unto it, Thou shalt* **love thy neighbour** *as thyself. On these two commandments*

hang all the law and the prophets (Matt. 22:36–40).

Traditional Christians say that this is the only commandment in the New Testament. I won't argue that, because the Messiah cited this directly from the Old Testament:

> *And thou shalt **love the LORD thy God** with all thine heart, and with all thy soul, and with all thy might* (Deut. 6:5). *Thou shalt not hate thy brother in thine heart: thou shalt in any wise rebuke thy neighbour, and not suffer sin upon him. Thou shalt not avenge, nor bear any grudge against the children of thy people, but thou shalt **love thy neighbour** as thyself: I am the LORD* (Lev. 19:17–18).

And He confirmed in Matthew 5:17 that He did not come to destroy any of these laws. What He quoted in Matthew 22:36–40 covers all of God's laws and commandments, the whole Torah. God's laws and commandments teach throughout the Torah of His unending love, mercy, and grace, and how He desires to conform us to that aspect of it (Rom. 8:29).

Look at what Luke wrote about Paul decades after the Messiah's resurrection: *And when they had appointed him a day, there came many to him into his lodging; to whom he expounded and testified the kingdom of God, persuading them concerning Jesus, both out of the law of Moses, and out of the prophets, from morning till evening* (Acts 28:23). Paul preached about salvation in the Messiah and about the kingdom of God from the Old Testament Scriptures. This is the Scripture from which Timothy was taught in his youth. Everything that is in the New Testament comes from the Old Testament. The sacrifice of the Messiah was a mystery to many and is revealed in the New Testament.

Most of today's professing Christians still don't understand the real truth about which laws the Messiah came to fulfill and how He fulfilled them.

As the Lamb of God, He fulfilled the animal sacrifices and ritualistic laws (read Heb. 7–10). Typical traditional church doctrines teach that this fulfilled everything that there is to be fulfilled, in a sense that He fulfilled God's commandments and laws by keeping them for us and then abolishing them. But there is much yet to be fulfilled, which is prophesied in the Old Testament. And once you know and believe this truth, you will see it all through the New Testament. That is the gospel of the kingdom of God of which the Messiah and the apostles preached, which can be understood only by studying the fulfillment of God's salvation plan as depicted by His Holy days of Leviticus 23 and Deuteronomy 16.

God wants us to learn His Holy, perfect, and unchanging ways: *And when Abram was ninety years old and nine, the LORD appeared to Abram, and said unto him, I am the Almighty God; walk before me, and **be thou perfect*** (Gen. 17:1). The Messiah cited it to His disciples: ***Be ye therefore perfect**, even as your Father which is in heaven is perfect* (Matt. 5:48). Peter preached it in the New Testament: *Because it is written, **Be ye holy**; for I am holy* (1 Peter 1:16). God's people are to become holy and perfect, just as it was required in the days of old. He has not changed His standards. How can we learn to walk with Him if He changes His ways? And His desire is to walk with us. How comforting and encouraging it is to know that He wants to walk with us. Hallelujah, praise His holy name! But we can't walk with Him if we deny and reject the very laws that define Him and His unchanging and perfect, holy character. And if His laws and commandments are burdensome, as proclaimed by traditional Christianity, then we should not even desire to walk with Him.

If you studied the Hebrew/Greek/English section at the beginning, you probably realized that, when the Scriptures talk about burdensome and grievous terms as being unbearable, it always refers to burdens that come from the laws and traditions of men, the rudiments and elements of this Satan-governed world, and not from God's laws. In Exodus we see that God promised to—now read this carefully—redeem His children from the Egyptian bondage and slavery: *Wherefore say unto the children of Israel, I am the LORD, and I will bring you **out from under the burdens** of the Egyptians, and I will **rid you out of their bondage**, and **I will redeem you** with a stretched out arm, and with great judgments* (Exod. 6:6). And God said after He redeemed them: *Ye have seen what I did unto the Egyptians, and how I bare you on eagles' wings, and brought you unto myself* (Exod. 19:4). Just as He offered liberty to the children of Israel in Exodus 6:6, He offers the same liberty for believers in Him today in the New Testament: *Come unto me, all ye that labour and are heavy laden, and I will give you rest. Take my yoke upon you, and learn of me; for I am meek and lowly in heart: and ye shall find rest unto your souls. For my **yoke is easy**, and **my burden is light*** (Matt. 11:28–30). He is obviously relating to how He took the Israelites out of Egypt. He said this before He was crucified, while still under the Old Testament sacrificial and ritualistic laws. God is a loving Father who cares for His children, wherefore He never imposes anything unbearable upon them (1 Cor. 10: 13).

Is this a yoke of bondage? Is God imposing a burden that is grievous to be borne? That's what the traditional church system has labeled obedience to God's commandments as being. If that be so, it sets up a serious contradiction in Scripture because God says *even* in the New Testament that His commandments are not grievous (1 John 5:2–3). Therefore, it deserves our unbiased and prayerful study with an open mind because Scriptures cannot contradict (John

10:35). To say that God's commandments are burdensome contradicts His Word. James has very encouraging words for God's commandments. He sees that liberty in them: *But whoso looketh into the **perfect law of liberty**, and continueth therein, he being not a forgetful hearer, but a **doer** of the work, this man shall be blessed in his deed* (James 1:25). He points out the excellence in them:

> *If ye **fulfil the royal law** according to the scripture, Thou shalt love thy neighbour as thyself, ye do well: But if ye have respect to persons, ye commit sin, and are convinced of the law as transgressors. For whosoever shall keep the whole law, and yet offend in one point, he is guilty of all. For he that said, Do not commit adultery, said also, Do not kill. Now if thou commit no adultery, yet if thou kill, thou art become a transgressor of the law. So speak ye, and so do, as they that shall be judged by the **law of liberty*** (James 2:8–12).

Paul preached the same principles: *For as many as have sinned without law shall also perish without law: and as many as have sinned in the law shall be judged by the law; For not the hearers of the law are just before God, but the doers of the law shall be justified* (Rom. 2:12–13).

We have trouble. Paul, the apostle who apparently said that there were no more laws, also said that the doers of the laws would be justified. How can this be? If I understand this correctly, lawless sinners will perish and law-abiding sinners will be judged by the law of liberty (James 2:12, above). Which one of these stands a chance for life? Remember what the Messiah said?—*If thou wilt enter into life, keep the commandments* (Matt. 19:17). While the chance is obviously zero for the lawless, the law-abider does stand a chance. It stands to reason because, if you abide by the law of God and happen to transgress it, God can convict you and, if you repent of it, He will forgive. This is the royal law of liberty, wherewith the Messiah has set us free from the penalty of sin. This is how the Messiah magnified the law and made it honorable (Isa. 42:21). Who are the lawless ones? The people who are not keeping God's commandments. God inspired the apostles to write these Scriptures decades after the resurrection of the Messiah, at which point the laws were apparently done away with according to traditional church doctrine.

We'll confirm yet more the real scriptural meanings of *bondage, burden, grievous, weak and beggarly, yoke of bondage, rudiments and elements of this world,* and such terms. We'll see that the Scriptures never refer to obedience to God's commandments when using these terms. And we'll also learn that God's laws and commandments truly are the perfect and royal laws of liberty by which law-abiding believers will be tried and measured.

5. Galatians: Justification

We will start with a phrase from the book of Galatians, the book that the traditional Christians quote notoriously to say that this is where the apostle Paul proves that the Lord did away with God's laws because, they say, those laws were a yoke of bondage, a phrase they use triumphantly and with great authority. These Christians have misled and deceived millions or perhaps billions of people by persuading them to believe that the Messiah did away with God's laws and commandments because, as Paul says in Galatians 5:1, they are a yoke of bondage, which makes them grievous, burdensome, and unbearable, wherefore we are now saved by grace, and grace alone—*Stand fast therefore in the liberty wherewith Christ hath made us free, and be not entangled again with the **yoke of bondage*** (Gal 5:1).

First off, we can see what Paul means by *yoke of bondage* and what laws he is referring to throughout the whole epistle. He explains it very well. He just finished explaining in Galatians 4:21–31 that we have a choice between bondage and liberty. He uses the Hagar-Ishmael old covenant (bondage) versus the Sarah-Isaac new covenant (liberty) allegory to address a very important point: justification, which is his emphasis throughout the

The Commandments of God

book of Galatians. And, as free moral agents, we must choose between bondage and freedom.

The animal sacrifices of the old covenant did not provide a direct means of justification from sin and death, because God did not design it to be able to take away sin: *For it is not possible that the blood of bulls and of goats should take away sins* (Heb. 10:4). Paul compares the old covenant with Hagar, because she gave birth to Ishmael, and with bondage to sin and death, because Ishmael was conceived and born by carnal means. On the other hand, he compares Sarah with the new covenant, because she gave birth to Isaac, and with liberty and freedom from sin and death, because Isaac was conceived and born by promise, which required the faith of Abraham and was thus a miracle from God.

It requires faith in the Messiah's sacrifice to have sins forgiven, whereby we become justified and whereby the death penalty is released, thus reconciling us to God. As we just read, the animal sacrifices of the old covenant, sometimes referred to as the law of Moses, did not have the provisions to take away sins, but the sacrifice of the Messiah of the new covenant does, as the law of the Messiah. Neither did the old covenant have the promise of eternal life, which is the better promise of the new covenant: *But now hath he obtained a more excellent ministry, by how much also he is the mediator of a better covenant, which was established upon better promises* (Heb. 8:6). *And this is the promise that he hath promised us, even eternal life* (1 John 2:25). The Holy Spirit was not available to the people in the days of Moses except to His messengers and prophets. God designed the old covenant in this way for a specific purpose, which was to physically train a habit of obedience into the hearts and minds of humans in order to become obedient to His spiritual and moral laws, the Ten Commandments. This was done by God providing physical and material blessings for obedience to His laws and physical and material punishments for disobedience

41

to them: *I call heaven and earth to record this day against you, that I have set before you life and death, blessing and cursing: therefore choose life, that both thou and thy seed may live* (Deut. 30:19; read Lev. 26 and Deut. 28).

In the days of old, whenever the Israelites broke God's commandments, they became guilty of the death penalty, the curse of the law, for which they had to do all the works of the law (animal sacrifices, rituals, and offerings), which could not take away the sins but reminded them of the urgent need of a Savior who would. This was to build up their faith in that promised Messiah: *But in those sacrifices there is a remembrance again made of sins every year* (Heb. 10:3, also Heb. 10:4, above).

And such a Savior was promised: *And I will put enmity between thee and the woman, and between thy seed and her seed; it shall bruise thy head, and thou shalt bruise his heel* (Gen. 3:15; Gal. 4:4), who would be delivered through the covenant that He made with their faithful father Abraham (Gen. 12:3; [Gen. 12–18]; Mat. 1:1), which was transferred to Isaac (Gen. 26; Mat. 1:2; Rom. 9:7; Gal. 4:28; Heb. 11:18) and then to Jacob, whose name God changed to *Israel* (Gen. 32:28, 35:9–12; Mat. 1:2; Acts 3:13); He was born in the tribe of Judah (Gen. 49:10; Mat.1:2; Luke 3:33–34); heir to David's throne (1 Ki. 2:33; Ps. 132:11; Jer. 23:5; Isa. 9:7; Mat. 1:1; Luke 1:32–33; John 7:42): *Hath not the scripture said, That Christ cometh of the seed of David, and out of the town of Bethlehem, where David was* (John 7:42)?; born of a virgin (Isa. 7:14; Luke 1:26–31). And the sacrificial and ritualistic laws did deliver them all guilty before God, *But the scripture hath concluded all under sin . . .* (Gal. 3:22), *For all have sinned, and come short of the glory of God* (Rom. 3:23), thus taking them to the faith of that promised Savior and Messiah:

> *Wherefore then serveth the **law** <nomos>?*[6]
> *It was added because of transgressions, till*

the seed should come to whom the promise was made; and it was ordained by angels in the hand of a mediator (Gal. 3:19). *But the scripture hath concluded all under sin . . .* (Gal. 3:22). *Wherefore the **law** <nomos>*[6] *was our schoolmaster to bring us unto Christ, that we might be justified by faith* (Gal.3:24).

I'll take some time here to confirm what part of the laws Paul is referring to. It's quite obvious that he's relating to the sacrificial and ritualistic laws that God had Moses write into a book: *For as many as are of the works of the law <nomos>*[6] *are under the curse: for it is written, Cursed is every one that continueth not in all things which are **written in the book of the law** <nomos>*[6] *to do them* (Gal. 3:10). Paul is not referring directly to the Ten Commandments here. The Ten Commandments were written into stone tablets with the finger of God: *And he gave unto Moses, when he had made an end of communing with him upon mount Sinai, two tables of testimony, tables of stone, **written with the finger of God*** (Exod. 31:18). These were placed ***inside*** the ark, which was under the mercy seat: *And I turned myself and came down from the mount, and put the tables **in the ark** which I had made . . .* (Deut. 10:5). The covenant and the additional laws were written in a book by Moses: *And it came to pass, when Moses had made an end of writing the words of this law **in a book** . . .* (Deut. 31:24). This was referred to as the book and law of Moses: *As Moses the servant of the LORD commanded the children of Israel, as it is written in the **book of the law of Moses** . . .* (Josh. 8:31). This book was placed ***in the side*** of the ark; not under the mercy seat: *Take this book of the law, and put it **in the side** of the ark . . .* (Deut. 31:26).

Whenever the Messiah and His apostles addressed the Ten Commandments, they used the Greek word <entole>.[7] Examples from Paul are 1 Corinthians 7:19 and Romans

7:12. In Romans 7:12, he used both <entole>[7] and <nomos>:[6] *Wherefore the law* <nomos>[6] *is holy, and the commandment* **<entole>[7]** *holy, and just, and good* (Rom. 7:12). Three decades after the Messiah's resurrection, Paul still called both the law <nomos>[6] and the commandment <entole>[7] holy. The Messiah clearly identified the commandments: *For laying aside the commandment* <entole>[7] *of God, ye hold the tradition of men . . .* (Mark 7:8). John used the same word: *For this is the* <agape>[1] *love of God, that we keep his commandments* <entole>[7] *. . .* (1 John 5:3). And this pattern is consistent.

The same laws are spoken of by Paul in Ephesians 2:15: *Having abolished in his flesh the enmity, even the law* <nomos>[6] *of commandments* <entole>[7] *contained in ordinances . . .* **<dogma>**.[8] *Dogma* means a civil, ceremonial, or ecclesiastical law. The Messiah abolished the ceremonial laws, the *'animal'* sacrificial and ritualistic system. He became our high priest whereby He replaced the Levitical priesthood of the ecclesiastical system (Heb. 7–9). There is no hint of the Messiah abolishing any of His moral laws.

It's very important to discern which laws are being referred to. It's obvious that Paul is not saying that you'll be cursed for obeying the Ten Commandments. What is clearly stated throughout all Scriptures is that we will be cursed for breaking them. And almost all of the time we will break them because we obey man's laws instead of God's. The apostles tell us whom we ought to obey: *Then Peter and the other apostles answered and said, We ought to obey God rather than men* (Acts 5:29). And mostly, these laws of men are commanded to be obeyed by traditional church doctrines.

Often we will hear traditional Christians explain away the need to obey God's commandments by stating that God required of us to keep His commandments before the crucifixion but that we are now justified by faith. Paul states clearly that justification had always come only through faith and that it never was any other way, and he quotes directly from the Old Testament Scriptures to prove that very point: *But that no man is justified by the law* <nomos>[6] *in the sight of God, it is evident: for,* **The just shall live by faith**. *And the* **law** <nomos>[6] *is not of faith: but, The man that doeth them shall live in them* (Gal. 3:11–12). Quoted from the Old Testament: *Behold, his soul which is lifted up is not upright in him: but* **the just shall live by his faith** (Hab. 2:4). *Ye shall therefore keep my statutes, and my judgments: which if a man do, he shall live in them: I am the LORD* (Lev. 18:5). God does not change His standards, but man has worked at changing them for about 6,000 years.

The curse of the law is the penalty for sin, from which the animal sacrifices could not free a man. Only faith in the Messiah's sacrifice redeems and heals us from that curse: *Christ hath redeemed us from the curse of the law* <nomos>,[6] *being made a curse for us: for it is written, Cursed is every one that hangeth on a tree* (Gal. 3:13). Through repentance, He redeems us from the curse, not from the law.

The sacrificial laws of the old covenant were added to work together with the Abrahamic covenant because of the Israelites' frequent sinning; thus it worked toward eventually circumcising their hearts, so that they could love Him from their heart:

> *Circumcise therefore the foreskin of your heart, and be no more stiffnecked* (Deut. 10:16). *And the LORD thy God will circumcise thine heart, and the heart of thy seed, to love the LORD thy God with all thine heart, and with all thy soul, that thou mayest live* (Deut. 30:6). *Circumcise yourselves to the LORD, and take away the foreskins of your heart . . .* (Jer. 4:4).

When we repent for breaking God's laws, turn to Him, and obey them, He imparts His Holy Spirit into our heart: *And we are his witnesses of these things; and so is also the Holy Ghost, whom God hath given **to them that obey him*** (Acts 5:32), whereby the heart becomes spiritually circumcised:

For he is not a Jew, which is one outwardly; neither is that circumcision, which is outward in the flesh: But he is a Jew, which is one inwardly; and circumcision is that of the heart, in the spirit, and not in the letter; whose praise is not of men, but of God (Rom. 2:28-29; cf. Col. 2:11; Phil. 3:3).

With the heart now circumcised, God sheds His love into it: *The love of God is shed abroad in our hearts by the Holy Ghost which is given unto us* (Rom. 5:5). Then we can love Him from our hearts.

By repenting of our sins, we are forgiven, by which we are justified, by God's grace, through our faith in the Messiah's sacrifice, which releases the death sentence (the curse of the law of Gen. 2:17; 3:3; Rom. 6:23). Thus the way is opened to enter into the new covenant. And Paul ends his allegory by reminding us how carnality, which resembles bondage to sin and death, wars against spirituality, which resembles freedom from that bondage. Therefore he urges us to cast out that carnality (bondwoman, animal sacrifices), which cannot justify, and to put on spirituality (free woman, the Messiah's sacrifice), which can justify, thus being released from that bondage to sin and death. We have to remember that an allegory does not address the actual issue but is a symbolic expression used to explain something in a deeper sense.

The animal sacrifices have become obsolete, rendered useless, because they have served their purpose (Heb. 9), which was to deliver us to the faith of the sacrifice of the promised Messiah (Gal. 3:24), so that the death penalty could be taken away, thus giving us His gift of eternal life

(Rom. 6:23). Today, just as in the days of Adam, Noah, and Moses, when we break God's commandments, we have sinned (1 John 3:4); so the law still charges us with the death penalty (Gen. 2:17; 3:3; Rom. 6:23), whereby we are enslaved into bondage to sin and death. This is the curse of the law. And faith in the Messiah's sacrifice frees us from that curse, which justifies us, thereby reconciling us to God—paid in full.

5a. Justification and Faith

The book of Galatians addresses mainly justification (forgiveness of sin, freedom from guilt) and faith in the Messiah (believing in His cleansing blood). True faith in and of the Messiah means that we acknowledge that we have sinned, broken God's commandments (Rom. 3:23; Gal. 3:22); wherefore we are due the death penalty (Gen. 2:17; 3:3; Rom. 6:23); and that there is absolutely no way out by our own means (bondage to sin and death), wherefore we must repent: *Except ye repent, ye shall all likewise perish* (Luke 13:3). *Repent ye therefore, and be converted, that your sins may be blotted out . . .* (Acts 3:19; cf. Isa. 55:7; 2 Chron. 7:14). To repent means to abhorrently regret and turn away from man's sinful ways and turn to God and His ways and ask Him for forgiveness. And we must accept His forgiveness and refrain from willful sinning. How do we refrain from sinning? There is only one way, and that is by sin's own definition: stop transgressing His laws (1 John 3:4). In plain words, repent of the past sins and stop transgressing God's law. This is faith in the Messiah's sacrifice.

This literally means that we have come to a point in our life where our sinful state has become unbearable; it has basically brought us to the end of the rope, as one might say. And this is what it takes to humble us in order that we acknowledge and admit our sins to God, because we want to be freed from them, cleared of that guilt, and released from the curse. This desire to be released of the guilt from sinning will cause us to surrender ourselves totally to God and pray to Him for forgiveness of those sins. Therefore, if we wholeheartedly believe and accept that the only way to escape the death sentence is to apply the blood of the sacrifice of the Messiah to those sins, the blood of the One who purchased us by dying on the tree to pay for them; believe that He died in our stead, took our curse upon Himself; and accept Him as our personal Lord and Savior from here forward and follow Him, then we have faith in the Messiah. Therefore, God will by His grace (undeserved and unearned), through our faith in the blood of the sacrifice of His Son, the Messiah, impute the Messiah's righteousness to us, whereby the sins are forgiven. Thus, we are justified, cleared of guilt, and freed from the death penalty, thereby reconciled to God the Father. This is the faith of the Messiah, which is the liberty wherewith He has set us free from the bondage to sin and death because faith in His sacrifice is the only way by which one may be justified for sins, and reconciled to God (Acts 4:12). Our justification in no way does away with our capability to sin but does give us the wonderful promise to have our sins forgiven when we do slip up: *If we confess our sins, he is faithful and just to forgive us our sins, and to cleanse us from all unrighteousness* (1 John 1:9).

This warrants a question: does this justification do away with the law that was transgressed, so that now we can break it without sinning or that we now cannot break it, even if we try, because it is done away? I know this sounds crazy, but that is what the "law-done-away" doctrines imply. Yes, it's true; the *animal* sacrificial laws are done away but not God's moral laws.

When the Messiah through His Father's love for us willingly offered up His body, sacrificing His sinless and blameless life and shedding His innocent blood for our sins, whereby He took our death sentence upon Himself, God was glorified. In like manner, we glorify God through the Messiah when we offer ourselves to sacrifice our life to His Son, that is, accepting to become a living sacrifice for Him, come out of this world and walk as He walked: *I beseech you therefore, brethren, by the mercies of God, that ye present your bodies a living sacrifice, holy, acceptable unto God, which is your reasonable service. And be not conformed to this world . . .* (Rom. 12:1–2). *Ye also, as lively stones, are built up a spiritual house, an holy priesthood, to offer up spiritual sacrifices, acceptable to God by Jesus Christ* (1 Peter 2:5). *He that saith he abideth in him ought himself also so to walk, even as he walked* (1 John 2:6). The Lord said, if your eye offends you, pluck it out. If your hand offends you, cut it off (Matt. 5:29–30). That's quite a sacrifice. We can see that the sacrifices and the circumcision have not been done away but have rather taken on a much higher meaning, thus demanding much more of us than before. We have become a living sacrifice for Him if we believe Him. He meant it when He said not one jot or tittle would pass from the law (Matt. 5:17–19).

We've gone over a couple of different scenarios that Paul uses in the book of Galatians to explain how one must be justified and that there is only that one way. He approaches the issue in many different ways in hopes that we will understand one scenario or another. Each scenario emphasizes solely on justification; the fact that circumcision, works of laws, and keeping God's laws, nothing that we do, can justify us from the guilt of past sin, because by these carnal means, the need of the Messiah's sacrifice is being left out, thus rendering the Savior's sacrifice of no effect. In other words, if we can be justified by any other means whatsoever, our Lord died in vain. If a sin is committed, that means that God's law has been broken, and the law that we broke cannot change anything we did except to convict and condemn us (Rom. 7:7). Only the righteous blood of the Messiah's sacrifice can heal it and take the curse away if we repent for breaking it.

Once we understand this truth clearly, the rest of the book of Galatians—and Romans, with which it parallels—becomes much easier to understand and makes a lot more sense because it removes the contradictions, allowing it to align with the rest of the Holy Scriptures. That's why it is so important that we clarify in each case how Paul uses the terms *law* and *circumcision* in his epistles. As we just saw in the previous section, he often uses *law* <nomos>[6] to relate to the sacrificial and ritualistic laws, sometimes called the law of Moses. Sometimes he will use the word *circumcision* in a similar manner. He frequently uses either or both of these words to point to all of the laws, which are syncretized with the Pharisaic laws and traditional doctrines and the penitent laws of the pagan Gnostics and ascetics (Col. 2:18–23). We see this throughout Paul's epistles and the book of Acts. It is extremely important to clarify the context in which it is being used in each case. Paul clearly shows that the Pharisees in Galatia were not keeping God's laws (Gal. 5–6), as also did the Messiah in John 7:19: *Did not Moses give you the law, and yet none of you keepeth the law?* They were putting the utmost importance into justification by means of circumcision, which obligated them to keep their

If sin really is the transgression of God's laws, and if those laws really are done away, then we cannot sin. It's that simple. And if that be so, why then are the preachers of these doctrines building so many big expensive churches in which to gather hordes of people to teach them not to sin? It just doesn't add up. These questions deserve honest answers.

syncretized package of laws: *For I testify again to every man that is* **circumcised**, *that he is a debtor to do the whole law. Christ is become of no effect unto you, whosoever of you are justified by the law* <nomos>;[6] *ye are fallen from grace* (Gal. 5:3–4). Here he used the word *circumcised* to mean the whole package of Pharisaic-Judaized laws.

Paul is not saying that everyone who is circumcised for whatever reason is bound to do the whole sacrificial and ritual law. He says that whoever gets circumcised for the reason that these perverted Pharisees were doing it is virtually rejecting the faith in the Messiah's sacrifice, thereby apostatizing His doctrine. No rite, no custom, and no observance of any laws can share the honor with the blood of the sacrifice of the Messiah. Trying to be justified by what we do is not of faith, therefore denying the grace of God, a grace that can only be applied through our faith in the sacrifice of the Messiah's blood. Paul is not talking about something that has changed at the crucifixion. He is addressing a centuries-old issue here, which is that the Pharisees were using man-made rituals, mixed with God's laws and commandments; pagan customs; and doctrines of penance to be justified by. And they had done it for centuries already, as is indicated throughout the Old Testament Scriptures. And He cut through that idea of being justified by those ways to teach them that that system never had and never would justify a man of his guilty past.

There is a great danger of taking this concept of justification by grace too far. What I mean is we need to obey God's commandments to be able to have His <agape>[1] love in our hearts, which is absolutely essential to be able to have faith in the Messiah's sacrifice. I will illustrate what I mean by clarifying another verse by which Protestants proclaim that, if we keep God's commandments, we cannot be justified:

> *Knowing that a man is not justified by the works* **<ergon>**[9] *of the law* <nomos>,[6] *but by the faith of Jesus Christ, even we have believed in Jesus Christ, that we might be justified by the faith of Christ, and not by the works* <ergon>[9] *of the law* <nomos>:[6] *for by the works* <ergon>[9] *of the law* <nomos>[6] *shall no flesh be justified* (Gal. 2:16).

Let's define what Paul is dealing with here. The word <ergon>[9] means *physical labor*, as toiling in occupation. We know what law <nomos>[6] he is referring to. He is obviously relating to the animal sacrifices, the rituals, and the offerings, which required daily and routine manual labor, which never did justify a man. And that is exactly what Paul is saying.

I want to clarify an important article at this point, which will hopefully make it easier for the remaining part of this book. The Pharisees and rabbis of that day did not accept our Lord and Savior as their promised Messiah who could take away the penalty of our sins. Therefore, they could not believe that He was the Lamb of God which was sent to become our Passover, thus replacing the animal sacrifices and the High Priest. They still performed the animal sacrificial and ritual ceremonies, and they did until the temple was destroyed in 70 AD. On top of the sacrificial laws, they had adopted many pagan customs and penance-motivated doctrines from the Gnostic and ascetic religions of the people whom they were proselytizing continually in nations around them. And proselytizing they were: *Woe unto you, scribes and Pharisees, hypocrites! for ye compass sea and land to make one proselyte, and when he is made, ye make him twofold more the child of hell than yourselves* (Matt. 23:15). According to the Messiah, not much good comes out of religious missionaries. And the

Pharisees and rabbis syncretized that garden variety of doctrines with God's laws and commandments. This is Judaism. These are the kind of people Paul was dealing with almost everywhere he took the gospel. We can be sure that the demonized doctrines from Simon the sorcerer were also mixed in with the Pharisaic doctrines and had penetrated the beliefs of the Galatian people because Paul claimed they were bewitched: *O foolish Galatians, who hath bewitched you . . .* (Gal. 3:1). According to Luke's record, Simon had bewitched all the people in the area of Samaria, which was the capital of many Israelites at the time, and also some Jews of that day:

> *But there was a certain man, called Simon, which beforetime in the same city used sorcery, and bewitched the people of Samaria, giving out that himself was some great one: To whom they all gave heed, from the least to the greatest, saying, This man is the great power of God. And to him they had regard, because that of long time he had bewitched them with sorceries* (Acts 8:9–11).

Luke says they all gave heed to his sorcery. Then the Pharisees topped that off with hundreds of traditions of their own, which they all together elevated to commandment status through the temple system. Yes, it really gets ugly. That must have been one mega-sized demon-driven package of laws that Paul had to contend with. So, whenever I mention Pharisaic or Judaized laws from here forward, you know what I'm referring to.

Of course, the Pharisees could see no other way of being justified than by performing circumcision and the works of that corrupted and perverted demon-driven system.

Anyone with an open mind knows that keeping the Ten Commandments <entole>[7] does not require any <ergon>[9] works. The people who make claims that keeping God's commandments cuts us off from God's grace because we cannot be justified by the works of the laws need to seriously rethink that concept, study the Scriptures, and believe what they find there.

Paul definitely had his work cut out for Him. He endured to the end, until they killed him, which was about one year before the temple was destroyed. The reason he could endure was because he had faith in the true Messiah of the true God of heaven and earth, wherefore the Holy Spirit dwelled in him and kept him strong in that faith. His humbleness and strong faith in the Messiah created in him the strength of the Messiah, whereby his burden was made light (Matt. 11:28–30). As he explains, it was the Messiah's strength in him that made him strong:

> *And lest I should be exalted above measure through the abundance of the revelations, there was given to me a thorn in the flesh, the messenger of Satan to buffet me, lest I should be exalted above measure. For this thing I besought the Lord thrice, that it might depart from me* (2 Cor. 12:7–8).

The thorn, whatever it was, was obviously bothersome, and that's how he was humbled:

> *And he said unto me, My grace is sufficient for thee: for my strength is made perfect in weakness. Most gladly therefore will I rather glory in my infirmities, that the power of Christ may rest upon me. Therefore I take pleasure in infirmities, in reproaches, in necessities, in persecutions, in distresses for Christ's sake:*

for when I am weak, then am I strong (2 Cor. 12:9-10).

And that is how he tore down demon-driven strongholds. And that faith can come only from and through the Messiah, by seeking to know Him and His ways and by becoming obedient to His ways. His ways are God's ways; and God's ways are by and through His <agape>[1] love. And that love is keeping God's commandments (1 John 5:3), which fulfills the laws (Rom. 13:8-10). Paul is in no way teaching against keeping God's commandments. Remember, there cannot be contradictions in the Scriptures, and we can see that there aren't any. He strictly reinforces that faith establishes law, upholding and supporting it: *Do we then make void the law through faith? God forbid: yea, we establish the law* (Rom. 3:31). He further confirms it: *The doers of the law shall be justified* (Rom. 2:13), through *faith which worketh by* <agape>[1] *love* (Gal. 5:6), which 1 John 5:3 explains: *For this is the love of God, that we keep his commandments . . .* James 2:17 reinforces that keeping (works) of them: *Even so faith, if it hath not works, is dead, being alone,* wherefore Paul says, *The love of God is shed abroad in our hearts by the Holy Ghost which is given unto us* (Rom. 5:5). Peter says to whom it is given: *And we are his witnesses of these things; and so is also the Holy Ghost, whom God hath given to them that obey him* (Acts 5:32). Salvation comes to those who have circumcised their hearts through obedience to Him: *And being made perfect, he became the author of eternal salvation unto all them that obey him* (Heb. 5:9).

Let's sum this up: Without the love of God, which develops from keeping God's commandments, faith is of no avail: it's dead. Faith works by and through <agape>[1] love, which is shed abroad in the hearts of those who obey God, by His grace, through faith in the sacrifice of the Messiah. To be able to have this faith, which is the faith of the Messiah and works through God's Love, we must faithfully keep His commandments. Faith is dead without works, just as works are dead without faith.

We will now go back to the start of the book of Galatians and confirm Paul's doctrinal sincerity in the issues we have hopefully clarified. We will start with his personal testimony and with the authentication of his apostleship for the Messiah:

> *For ye have heard of my conversation in time past in the **Jews' religion**, how that beyond measure I persecuted the church of God, and wasted it: And profited in the Jews' religion above many my equals in mine own nation, being more exceedingly zealous of the **traditions of my fathers** (Gal. 1:13–14; see also Phil. 3).*

Paul warns Titus of the same traditions:

> *Not giving heed to **Jewish** fables, and **commandments of men**, that turn from the truth. Unto the pure all things are pure: but unto them that are defiled and unbelieving is nothing pure; but even their mind and conscience is defiled. They profess that they know God; but **in works they deny him**, being abominable, and disobedient, and unto every good work reprobate (Titus 1:14–16).*

The traditions that we just studied are what the Messiah blatantly condemns the Pharisees for in Matthew 15 and 23 and Mark 7. We will review that account in Mark:

> *For the Pharisees, and all the Jews, except they wash their hands oft, eat not, holding the*

tradition of the elders. And when they come from the market, except they wash, they eat not. And many other things there be, which they have received to hold, as the washing of cups, and pots, brasen vessels, and of tables. Then the Pharisees and scribes asked him, Why walk not thy disciples according to the tradition of the elders, but eat bread with unwashen hands? He answered and said unto them, Well hath Esaias prophesied of you hypocrites, as it is written, This people honoureth me with their lips, but their heart is far from me. Howbeit in vain do they worship me, teaching for doctrines the commandments **<entalma>**[11] *of men. For laying aside the commandment <entole>*[7] *of God, ye hold the* **tradition of men,** *as the washing of pots and cups: and many other such like things ye do. And he said unto them, Full well ye reject the commandment of God, that ye may keep your own tradition* (Mark 7:3–9). **Making the word of God of none effect through your tradition,** *which ye have delivered: and many such like things do ye* (Mark 7:13).

Please read Mathew 15 and 23 and John 5–10, where the Messiah goes into intense detail as He excoriates the scribes and Pharisees. Notice in verses 3 and 5 above that the traditions are of the religious Pharisees, the Jewish fathers and elders. We need to establish clearly in our minds and bear in mind throughout the remainder of this book that these are the same traditions that Paul had come out of.

The Pharisees, and Paul before he was converted, had a zeal for God, and they thought that they were doing the right thing and pleasing God:

> *For I bear them record that they have a zeal of God, but not according to knowledge. For they being ignorant of God's righteousness, and going about to establish their own righteousness, have not submitted themselves unto the righteousness of God* (Rom. 10:2–3).

The Messiah warned His disciples of the dangerous results of such a prideful and self-righteous mentality: *Whosoever* [the Pharisees; religious leaders] *killeth you will think that he doeth God service* (John 16:2). On these grounds is how the Pharisees eventually executed the Messiah and His disciples. They thought they were following God's orders.

One has to wonder if Paul was among that group of Pharisees when the Messiah excoriated them in Mark 7. There is no mention of such, but Paul makes it clear in numerous Scriptures that he came from such a sect of Pharisees and that he was very zealous of those traditions of his fathers: *After the most straitest sect of our religion I lived a Pharisee* (Acts 26:5; read also Acts 23:6; Phil. 3:5).

Paul makes it abundantly clear throughout the book of Galatians that the people were keeping a variety of laws from many different religions, a combination of pagan, gnostic, ascetic, and Jewish (Pharisaic), which were all syncretized together with God's commandments into one demon-driven mega-law doctrinal system, by which they were justifying themselves by their own traditional standards. This package of laws is often called *Judaism*, referring to the Judaized version of God's commandments. Paul explains that they were backbiting and hating each other (Gal. 5:15, 19–21), which can come only from the enslavement to man's laws. Then he follows up as to how they should love and treat one another (Gal. 5:22–6:2), which will develop from keeping God's laws. He goes on to list many of the important things that they should and should not be doing. Study it and you will understand.

Paul's concern was that the Galatian people were being persuaded by the same sect of Pharisees that we read about in Mark 7 to get them circumcised and get them to keep their laws. The Pharisaic Jews and proselytes (Gentiles converted to Judaism) were bad-mouthing Paul to the Galatian people (Gal. 1:6–9) in order to persuade them to become justified by their religious standards for their honor and glory. They would have to be circumcised, which was their sign, their proof that they were being justified by their standards, which obligated them to keep their Judaized package of laws. Their laws contained God's laws, but as the Messiah clarified in Mark 7, their traditions caused God's commandments to be forsaken. This is the same package of laws that Paul frequently refers to as circumcision or laws, as we already learned earlier. His use of the term *circumcision* here indicates the signature to the contract of the Pharisaic package of laws. Sometimes he will refer to them as *the Pharisee's laws, traditions of my fathers and elders, philosophy and vain deceit, after the traditions of men, rudiments and elements of this world, worthless worship*, and *not after the Lord*.

This Pharisaic system, with which they were perverting the Galatian people, concerned Paul severely because he knew exactly what that system was all about, as he just finished explaining that he at one time had been a champion and leader of that very system. He used his testimony for an example to get them to understand that he knew what he was talking about. Therefore they would hopefully understand that they were getting into exactly the same traditional system he had come out of.

Paul keeps preaching that the only way one can be freed from the death penalty is to be forgiven for the sins by God's grace, through faith in the sacrifice of the Messiah. As the Messiah and Paul confirm to the Pharisees, their traditional doctrines rendered their worship worthless and in vain.

These are very strong and sobering words from the Messiah. Do we really understand what He is saying in Mark 7? He says that people do worship Him in vain. How can it be that worshipping Him can be in vain? Is it possible that, for example, when we are keeping certain pagan traditions, like keeping pagan holidays as holy days and Sunday as the Lord's sanctified Sabbath day, and so on, we could be doing just that? Could we be deceived into worshipping another messiah than the Messiah who was crucified for keeping His Father's commandments and tells us to do the same (John 15:10)?

When confronted about such pagan traditions, do we not quickly defend it and justify it by stating that we are doing it for the Messiah and not for Baal? The Messiah said that they were worshipping Him in vain by obeying the doctrines and traditions of men whereby they were forsaking God's commandments. Think about it. He did not leave any room to justify any of their traditions or doctrines, did He? Neither did He leave any doubt as to the importance of keeping the commandments of God. It is absolutely clear that God commands us to keep His commandments, and He clearly accepts none of man's traditions as worthy of worship. Period.

As humans, we like to think that God will be pleased by whatever, whoever, however, and whenever we worship as long as we profess with our lips that we are doing it in the Messiah's name. I want to compare this philosophy with an account from the time of Moses. When Moses was up on the mountain receiving more instructions from God, the Israelites built a golden calf from their jewelry. They even built an altar and sacrificed to the calf **in the name of the LORD**: *And when Aaron saw it, he built an altar before it; and Aaron made proclamation, and said, Tomorrow is a **feast to the LORD**. And they rose up early on the morrow, and offered burnt offerings, and brought peace offerings; and the people sat down to eat and to drink, and rose up* *to play.* (Exod. 32:5–6). Aaron declared it a 'Feast to the LORD'. They did it in the name of the God of Abraham. This violated the first four commandments: 1)They worshipped another god; not the One who delivered them out of Egypt. 2)They made an image to represent their god. 3)They used the LORD's name in vain. 4)They invented their own sabbath and feast day for worship. For this sin, God was determined to wipe them off the face of this earth (verse 10). Why, if they were doing it in His name? How will God justify today's traditional Christians who celebrate pagan holidays and worship days like Easter, Christmas, and Sunday in the name of the LORD? Think about it.

You be the judge of that, after you review and study the following Scriptures, where Paul addresses exactly that very issue in the New Testament. Paul also uses very strong language regarding exactly such idol worship, and it harmonizes perfectly with what the Messiah said. And Paul understood what He meant because he was converted from exactly that system.

It is interesting how non-Christians will make every effort to avoid the customs of Christians. On the other hand, professing Christians seem to take pleasure and great pride in observing pagan customs. This is done for fear of persecution, wherefore we are willing to believe, support, and obey whatever lies are necessary to justify this avoidance of persecution. And we justify it by labeling pagan customs with a Christian-flavored description and then elevating them to commandment status through church doctrines (feast to the LORD, [Exod. 32:5-6]).

Paul warns us how Satan presents himself as an angel of light and that he trains his ministers as ministers of righteousness in order to deceive us into believing that we are worshipping the true God while we bow down to his Christian-flavored doctrines and commandments, just as Eve did:

> *But I fear, lest by any means, as the serpent beguiled Eve through his subtilty, so your minds should be corrupted from the simplicity <**haplotes**>[12] that is in Christ. For if he that cometh preacheth **another** Jesus, whom we have not preached, or if ye receive another spirit, which ye have not received, or another gospel, which ye have not accepted, ye might well bear with him (2 Cor. 11:3–4). For such are false apostles, deceitful workers, transforming themselves into the apostles of Christ. And no marvel; for Satan himself is **transformed into an angel of light**. Therefore it is no great thing if his ministers also be **transformed as the ministers of righteousness**; whose end shall be according to their works (2 Cor. 11:13–15). Simplicity means 'non self-seeking singleness.'*

Once we are made aware of such a truth, Paul commands us to unyoke from such a lawless system and have nothing in common with them:

> *But now I have written unto you not to keep company, if any man that is called a brother be a fornicator, or covetous, or an **idolater**, or a railer, or a drunkard, or an extortioner; with such an one no not to eat (1 Cor. 5:11).*

> *Be ye not unequally yoked together with unbelievers: for what fellowship hath righteousness with **unrighteousness <anomia>**[10]? and what communion hath light with darkness? And what concord hath Christ with Belial? or what part hath he that believeth with an infidel? And what agreement*

hath the temple of God with idols? for ye are the temple of the living God; as God hath said, I will dwell in them, and walk in them; and I will be their God, and they shall be my people. Wherefore **come out** *from among them, and* **be ye separate***, saith the Lord, and touch not the* **unclean** <akathartos>[13] *thing; and I will receive you, And will be a Father unto you, and ye shall be my sons and daughters, saith the Lord Almighty* (2 Cor. 6:14-18).

Revelation 18:4 confirms the same thing: *And I heard another voice from heaven, saying,* **Come out of her***, my people, that ye be not partakers of her sins, and that ye receive not of her plagues* (Rev. 18:4). Notice that the word 'akathartos' is the same word Peter used in Acts 10:14 when he rebuked the unclean animals. It is also used in Revelations 18:2 as foul <akathartos>[13] spirit and unclean <akathartos>[13] bird.

The word *anomia* is translated in the New Testament of the King James Version as *iniquity* eleven times, as *unrighteousness* once, and as *transgression of the law* three times, each time to mean *lawlessness.*

What Paul addressed in 2 Corinthians parallels perfectly with what the Messiah said to the Pharisees. They were worshipping God in vain, by and through their traditions, by which they forsook God's commandments. Satan does not necessarily sneak in through the backdoors and cracks. That would not be deceiving. He mixes truth with lies and comes disguised as the true light. Paul has a colorful way of detailing how Satan penetrates church doctrines with his version of messiah, through whom he does it. According to these Scriptures, such an apostasy would come from the pulpit. I challenge you to find out where such days as Easter, Christmas, and Sunday have originated from and to see how Satan has used the traditional church system to flavor paganism with God's Word to make it appear as though it is coming from God. You might be shocked if and when you find the truth of it.

As the Messiah said, they were forsaking God's commandments by their traditions, which in the Holy Scriptures are called idolatry, which to God is adultery:

> *Wherefore, my dearly beloved, **flee from idolatry** (1 Cor. 10:14). But I say, that the things which the Gentiles sacrifice, they sacrifice to devils, and not to God: and I would not that ye should have fellowship with devils. Ye cannot drink the cup of the Lord, and the cup of devils: ye cannot be partakers of the Lord's table, and of the table of devils (1 Cor. 10:20-21; read also Jer. 10).*

Now read again 2 Corinthians 6:16–18 and Revelations 18:4, and you will see how urgently God is calling His people out of the pagan Babylonian system: Read Revelation 17–18 and Isaiah 47 to see which system God is calling His people out of. It is clearly a religious church system that is entangled with Babylonianism.

We cannot worship God and Satan at the same time. Once God dwells in us, Satan must go. I don't mean that Satan has to go only because of God's Spirit being in our hearts, but that we must see to it that we will not willfully do those things that will give Satan an opportunity to enter into our lives or hearts. Heeding to any pleasures and lusts of the world will invite Satan in. This is sin. As Paul said in 2 Corinthians 6:16, we are God's temple. Remember that God made us free moral agents. He says that He will not choose for us, but we must choose whom we will serve. As Elijah said, it will be one or the other, but certainly not both. *How long halt ye between two opinions? if the LORD be God, follow him: but if Baal, then follow him* (1 Kings 18:21). Read 1

Samuel 8 where it shows that God allows us to choose but warns that to be ruled by man is guaranteed bondage to slavery. The tragedy is, as God said to Samuel, if we choose the king of the nation, He will not hear our prayers, of which accounts like Nehemiah 5 are a testimony.

When I read such accounts I think of the situation in which USA and Canada are in today.

God says in Deuteronomy 30:19: *I call heaven and earth to record this day against you, that I have set before you life and death, blessing and cursing: therefore choose life, that both thou and thy seed may live.* The Messiah quoted it in Matthew 6:24: *No man can serve two masters: for either he will hate the one, and love the other; or else he will hold to the one, and despise the other.* **Ye cannot serve God and mammon.** Matthew 19:17: *If thou wilt enter into life, keep the commandments.* James and Paul say the same: *Ye adulterers and adulteresses, know ye not that the friendship of the world is enmity with God? whosoever therefore will be a friend of the world is the enemy of God* (James 4:4). There is no such thing as riding the fence. We choose one side or the other: *Let not sin therefore reign in your mortal body, that ye should obey it in the lusts thereof* (Rom. 6:12). *Know ye not, that to whom ye yield yourselves servants to obey, his servants ye are to whom ye obey; whether of sin unto death, or of obedience unto righteousness?* (Rom. 6:16). (Life and death/blessing and cursing; sin unto death/obedience unto righteousness.) We MUST choose, LIFE or DEATH!

> We will obey either the pagan gods, death and cursing
> *OR*
> the eternal God, life and blessings, whichever we yield
> ourselves to.
> It will be one or the other. It cannot be both,
> Neither can it be none. One or the other it will be.

Paul brings out a strong point, which is the period of sanctification, training to walk in obedience to God's laws, while weaning off of the lustful ways of the world. Just as it took the children of Israel the complete generation to become sanctified, it will take us the rest of our lives, however long we yet may live, to learn to walk in His ways and to worship only Him to become sanctified (set apart, consecrated, and made holy) before Him. The common belief, that once we accept the Messiah into our hearts our eternity is then secured, is not supported by Scripture. We are not saved until we are in God's kingdom. Once we are there, yes, then we will be saved forever, which is salvation (deliverance, victory). If it was like the once-saved belief, why then would the Messiah and His apostles give us such strong warnings, such as hold on steadfastly, endure to the end, and not to turn or fall away from God's truth **after** having known it?

> *For we are made partakers of Christ, if we hold the beginning of our confidence stedfast **unto the end** (Heb. 3:14). For it is impossible for those **who were once** enlightened, and have tasted of the heavenly gift, and were made partakers of the Holy Ghost, And have tasted the good word of God, and the powers of the world to come, If they shall fall away, to renew them **again** unto repentance; seeing they*

crucify to themselves the Son of God afresh, and put him to an open shame (Heb. 6:4–6). *For if we sin wilfully **after** that we have received the knowledge of the truth, there remaineth no more sacrifice for sins* (Heb. 10:26). *For if after they have escaped the pollutions of the world through the knowledge of the Lord and Saviour Jesus Christ, they are **again entangled** therein, and overcome, the latter end is worse with them than the beginning. For it had been better for them not to have known the way of righteousness, than, **after they** have known it, to turn from the holy commandment delivered unto them. But it is happened unto them according to the true proverb, The dog is turned to his own vomit again; and the sow that was washed to her wallowing in the mire* (2 Peter 2:20–22). In other words, turning back to our traditions; our old ways.

The Messiah sums it up in very simple terms: *But he that shall **endure unto the end**, the same shall be saved* (Matt. 24:13). I have some questions for the "law-done-away" believers: If the laws are done away, how can one fall away from the truth by sinning? How can one sin, willfully or otherwise? Are these warnings just simply babble talk, or do they mean what they say? We must choose whom to believe; Scripture (every word of God [Deut. 8:3; Matt. 4:4]), or the 'lawless' preachers.

These warnings about Christians falling away after knowing the truth do not leave much argument for the once-saved/always-saved doctrine, do they? Again, this is the sanctification period in which the "law-done-away" once-saved people hate enough that they have indoctrinated whatever lies it takes to explain it away altogether. How is this done? Just as the Pharisees did it. Bury God's commandments <entole>[7] under man's commandments <entalma>[11], and they are rendered forsaken, done away (Mark 7). It's just that simple.

The forty-year journey from Egypt to Canaan was the Israelites' period of sanctification, and that was where they failed miserably, wherefore most of them perished in the wilderness. Of the few million people who literally left Egypt with Moses, the only two who endured the forty-year journey to Canaan were Joshua and Caleb. The faith the children of Israel had in the God of Abraham justified them from the Egyptian bondage and slavery to sin, but they did not keep that faith in that God; not enduring to the end (Matt. 24:13). They kept falling away to worship pagan gods. It got to a point where they feared the Lord while worshipping pagan gods. This sounds so familiar. When questioned why we observe and worship pagan holidays, do we not say that we are doing it for the Messiah and not for Baal? (Read Exod. 32:5-6; Exod. 34:11-17; Deut. 12:28–13:11; Judg. 2; 1 Sam. 8; 2 Kings 17; Jer. 10; Eze. 8; 7-18; 1 Cor. 10:1-14; 2 Cor. 6:14-18; and Heb. 4:2.)

In Galatians 4:3 and 4:8–10, Paul explains the heathen system from which the Galatians, who were heathen, had recently severed. This is yet another approach to help the Galatians to understand that the sacrifice of the Messiah was being left out. Paul explained the heathen, and the ritual system, in hopes that they would understand that God's laws of liberty were the only laws that mattered and that any other laws were absolutely worthless. *Even so we, when we were children, were in **bondage under the elements of the world** (Gal. 4:3).*

He again mentions bondage and the elements of the world; which are of this Satan-ruled world, mixed with the 'Pharisaical' rituals, through which Satan was the father of the Pharisees: *Ye are of your father the devil, and the lusts of your father ye will do. He was a murderer from the beginning, and abode not in the truth, because there is no truth in him. When he speaketh a lie, he speaketh of his own: for he is a liar, and the father of it* (John 8:44). These were the fathers and elders also of Paul and Peter as they testify in many Scriptures. And according to these Scriptures, this might apply to all traditionalists.

> *Satan will never tell the truth,*
> *unless it is a setup for a lie.*

Paul reminds the people of Galatia about those heathen-pagan ways that they had followed before he converted them:

> *Howbeit then, when ye knew not God, ye did service unto them which by nature are no gods. But now, after that ye have known God, or rather are known of God, how **turn ye again** to the weak and beggarly elements, whereunto ye desire again to be in bondage? Ye observe days, and months, and times, and years* (Gal. 4:8–10).

This phrase (and verse 3) is being used by the Protestant system in such a way as if Paul had severed them from God's laws and commandments earlier, thus implying that he is now afraid that they will go back to keeping them again. This is what the traditional Christians need it to mean to support their "law-done-away" doctrines. Remember what Paul said in Romans 8:7: *The carnal mind is enmity against God: for it is not subject to the law of God.* Mankind hates rules and laws, especially when coming from God, because we don't like authoritative rules. We like them to be very flexible, and un-authoritative; ear-tickling (2 Tim. 4:3-4). Paul says that this is a true test of spirituality: if we don't love God's laws, we are yet thinking carnally. If we love them, they are in us. If we hate the laws, we inevitably hate their giver. We will always say that we love God, right? But if we hate and reject His laws, our love for the Lawgiver cannot be true: *And hereby we do know that we know him, if we keep his commandments. He that saith, I know him, and keepeth not his commandments, is a liar, and the truth is not in him* (1 John 2:3–4).

By calling God's laws weak and beggarly elements of the world, traditional Christians imply that Paul, God's apostle, is a hypocrite. That would be about as close as it can get to blasphemy for Paul to label God's moral and spiritual laws and commandments as such, the same laws that he said must be kept because they are holy, just, and good, wherefore the doers of them would be justified. Does Paul contradict himself? Absolutely not. He's addressing post-Gentile people. It's clear that he's not referring to God's laws and commandments or His holy days. He said, before they knew God, they were doing service to the gods which were not gods by nature, which could be only pagan gods. These people did not know God before their conversion, wherefore they would not have known of God's commandments, laws, or holy days.

God condemns observing times. Nowhere does He condemn the keeping of His Holy days and Sabbaths but commands us to keep them. Neither does He call the keeping of them as observing times. Surely Paul cannot be condemning the keeping of God's Holy days, as billions are taught to believe. He kept them as the Lord taught him. It is obvious that Paul is talking about observing times and the pagan holidays of old. Paul referred to Leviticus 19 and Deuteronomy 18 when he summarized Galatians 4:10.

> *Ye shall not eat any thing with the blood: neither shall ye use enchantment, **nor observe times*** (Lev. 19:26). *Therefore shall ye observe all my statutes, and all my judgments, and do them: I*

am the LORD (Lev. 19:37). *There shall not be
found among you any one that maketh his son
or his daughter to pass through the fire, or that
useth divination, or an **observer of times**, or an
enchanter, or a witch* (Deut. 18:10). *For these
nations, which thou shalt possess, hearkened
unto **observers of times**, and unto diviners: but
as for thee, the LORD thy God hath not suffered
thee so to do* (Deut. 18:14).

Paul knew how God hated for the people to celebrate pagan deities.

There are a few Scriptures that some will quote in an effort to prove that God no longer wants His holy days observed. One that is frequently cited is Isaiah 1:14: *Your new moons and your appointed feasts my soul hateth: they are a trouble unto me; I am weary to bear them.* Read the whole chapter, and you will see that God was fed up with the way they were trying to worship Him by and through pagan deities. That's why He says **your** *new moons* and **your** *appointed feasts*. This was after the account of the golden calf (Exod. 32:5-6). Later people like Jeroboam put their gods in the temple and changed the timing of God's feast and worship days:

> *So he offered upon the altar which he had made
> in Bethel the fifteenth day of the eighth month,
> even in the month which he had **devised of
> his own heart**; and ordained a feast unto the
> children of Israel: and he offered upon the
> altar, and burnt incense* (1 Kings 12:33).

Jeroboam made priests of non-Levites; from people which were classified as the lowest people (verse 31). God hated their own devising of the timing of His feast days and their own ideas of gods to worship and their selecting of forbidden people to serve as His priests. That's what angered God. I believe that He had the modern-day Christian holidays and worship days in mind, most of which were already being celebrated during that time.

God had Isaiah write about 'your' new moons and 'your' appointed feasts about 600 BC. About 630 years later, the Messiah still practiced the 'Feasts of the LORD' and 'His' Sabbaths as God calls them: *Speak unto the children of Israel, and say unto them, Concerning the **feasts of the LORD**, which ye shall proclaim to be holy convocations, even these are **my feasts**. Six days shall work be done: but the seventh day is the sabbath of rest, an holy convocation; ye shall do no work therein: it is the **sabbath of the LORD** in all your dwellings. These are the **feasts of the LORD**, even holy convocations, which ye shall proclaim in their seasons* (Lev. 23:2–4). God calls the weekly and annual Sabbaths **'HIS'** days and feasts, and half a century after the resurrection, the apostles still practiced them.

I want to add a few notes to show where today's church traditions come from. Most Protestant preachers are trained by traditional orthodox theologians, who feast on commentaries and philosophies of traditional men like Plato, Constantine, Martin Luther, and so forth (see inset below). The philosophies of these men have greatly influenced the knowledge upon which the curriculum of Bible schools, Bible colleges, seminaries, and universities, and public schools have been established. This goes back to the early church fathers of many centuries ago who turned those pagan and traditional philosophies into church doctrines by elevating them to commandment status through the traditional church system, just as the Pharisees and rabbis did. These are of the same traditions that the Messiah and His apostles condemn throughout the Scriptures. And thanks be to God for making known in His Holy Scriptures that the doctrines and commandments that they are condemning are the man-made ones, and not His laws and commandments.

==

(INSET: Food For Thought)

I challenge traditional Christians to research the history and origin of the teachings of the early church fathers upon which the foundation of today's traditional church doctrines is established. You will find that many of the traditional church doctrines come from pre-Christian Greek philosophers who founded their beliefs upon Egyptian and Babylonian philosophies. Compare those beliefs with the doctrines of your church and then with the Holy Scriptures. If you're honestly searching for the truth, you may be shocked.

A few of the common and popular philosophers are: Socrates (470-399 BC); Plato (427–347 BC); Aristotle (384–322 BC); Virgil (70–19 BC); Origin (185–254 AD); Tertullian (160–230 AD); Constantine (280–337 AD). *(names from the Herbert W. Armstrong College Bible Correspondence Course).* Information about these philosophers and others like them can be found in most encyclopedias and also other resources. These philosophers all taught the immortality of the soul doctrines, upon which many non-Scriptural witchcraft doctrines are founded, which most of today's traditional churches use for their doctrines.

Forefather and Emperor Constantine I the Great took the liberty of pounding off the LORD's Sabbath for Sunday in about 321 AD, and the LORD's Passover for the pagan Easter in about 327 AD. Both of these edicts were founded upon his extreme 'anti-Jew' mentality, and were decreed as Holy Scriptural Canons by later Emperors by 367 AD. This can be found in the book: *Nicene and Post-Nicene Fathers, volume 14, 2ⁿᵈ series, published by 'Hendrickson' Publishers.*

When Martin Luther (1483–1546 AD) started the reformation in 1517 AD, he held on very tightly to many of the Romanized pagan doctrines of the Roman Catholic system from which he severed. His futile attempt to eradicate the 'immortal soul' doctrines was soon forgotten by the Protestant theologians. Like his forefather Constantine, Luther was also extremely 'anti-Jew', which is reflected in his teachings and passed on to the Protestant church system.

Because of the extreme 'anti-Jew' mentality, combined with the belief that the Old Testament is not binding upon the New Testament church, and the belief that the Ten Commandments were given only for the Jews; the doctrines of these forefathers are accordingly extremely 'anti-Torah'. Therefore, any doctrine which requires obedience to the Ten Commandments is labeled as 'Jewish' and as such is not to be used by the New Testament church.

If you've been deceived by this lie, remember that the Messiah and His apostles were born Jews! The apostles kept the LORD's Sabbaths and holy days with Gentiles decades after the Messiah's resurrection. End-time prophecies promise great wrath for people from all nations (Jew and Gentile) who call Him LORD and are not keeping the LORD's weekly and annual Sabbaths (Isa. 56:1–6; 66:22–23; Zech. 14:16–19).

===

5b. Acts 14: Heathenism in Lystra, Galatia

We will read a portion of Acts 14 to get a clearer understanding of why Paul is so suspicious that these people will turn again to worshipping the heathen-pagan gods and the planetary gods whom they worshipped before he converted them. That is what the people in Lystra, a city in the province of Galatia, were going to do. I am showing a map to help understand that Galatia, in modern-day Turkey, was a large province. In the book of Acts, Luke has recorded many struggles that Paul had in some of the cities and towns in Galatia. Most of the battles he encountered that had anything to do with the heathen-pagan and Gnostic practices occurred in this province.

These people were going to do sacrifices to Paul and Barnabas because, after Paul healed a sick man there, they thought that their pagan planetary gods had come down from the planets and stars to help them. They thought that Paul and Barnabas were their gods. We can see that these people would have had a strong enough faith to move mountains if that faith had been in the eternal God of heaven and earth instead of the pagan gods, wherefore their worship and sacrifice was totally and absolutely in vain. Please bear this in mind as we read this portion of Scripture:

> *And there sat a certain man at Lystra, impotent*
> *in his feet, being a cripple from his mother's*

*womb, who never had walked: The same heard Paul speak: who stedfastly beholding him, and perceiving that he had faith to be healed, Said with a loud voice, Stand upright on thy feet. And he leaped and walked. And when the people saw what Paul had done, they lifted up their voices, saying in the speech of Lycaonia, The gods are come down to us in the likeness of men. And they called Barnabas, Jupiter; and Paul, Mercurius, because he was the chief speaker. Then the priest of Jupiter, which was before their city, brought oxen and garlands unto the gates, and would have done sacrifice with the people. Which when the apostles, Barnabas and Paul, heard of, they rent their clothes, and ran in among the people, crying out, And saying, Sirs, why do ye these things? We also are men of like passions with you, and preach unto you that ye should turn from these vanities unto the living **God, which made heaven, and earth, and the sea, and all things that are therein**: Who in times past suffered all nations to walk in their own ways. Nevertheless he left not himself without witness, in that he did good, and gave us rain from heaven, and fruitful seasons, filling our hearts with food and gladness. And with these sayings scarce restrained they the people, that they had not done sacrifice unto them. And there came thither certain Jews from Antioch and Iconium, who persuaded the people, and having stoned Paul, drew him out of the city, supposing he had been dead* (Acts 14:8–19).

I trust that this will help to clarify what is in question in Galatians 4. Paul cannot be afraid of these people going back to observing God's laws, because that is not where they were before he converted them. Therefore, he cannot be condemning them for keeping God's feast (or holy) days. Notice how Paul identifies the eternal God of heaven and earth (verse 15) by exactly the same principles God says He is to be identified by in the fourth commandment: *For in six days the LORD made heaven and earth, the sea, and all that in them is, and rested the seventh day: wherefore the LORD blessed the sabbath day, and hallowed it* (Exod. 20:11).

Paul is clearly condemning the observing of the holidays and worship days from the heathen-pagan system, of which many are still commanded to be observed by today's traditional church system.

On Sunday the heathen people worshipped the sun god; on Monday they worshipped the moon god; on Tuesday, Mars, the god of war; on Wednesday, Mercury; on Thursday, Jupiter, the god of thunder; on Friday, Frigga, the fertility goddess of the sky; on Saturday, Saturn. Look them up in your encyclopedia. These are merely a few examples, only the days of the week. They had hundreds more in honor of almost anything and everything that you can think of. Look up the Roman holidays under *Festivals* in any reputable encyclopedia. You will find information on celebrations like December 25, a day on which they celebrated the rebirth of the "venerable" sun-god Mithras, centuries before the Messiah was born. Paul knew that these were the type of demon-driven pagan holidays that these people were accustomed to celebrating for the heathen gods.

Luke recorded that the Ephesians had the same troubles with Gnosticism and paganism: *And when the townclerk had appeased the people, he said, Ye men of Ephesus, what man is there that knoweth not how that the city of the Ephesians is a worshipper of the great goddess Diana, and of the image which fell down from Jupiter?* (Acts 19:35). Study this whole chapter with the commercial gains in mind, which come from the celebrating of days, times, and seasons like Christmas, Easter, Halloween/All Saints' Day, and so forth.

Paul is abhorred by their observing of the days, times, months, and years of the traditional pagan calendar, many of which today's traditional Christians are still keeping holy. These would be occasions like New Year's, Three Kings Day, Lent, Good Friday, Easter, sunrise service, Halloween/All Saints' Day, Christmas, Sunday, and a whole horde of other pagan days and festivals, too many to mention here; but these are the common and most accepted ones by traditional Christians. Each and every one of these holidays comes flavored with a Christian-like name and description to make us believe that they are from God. But the origin of these holidays is based on either a star, planet, or some Gnostic Baal god. All were, and still are, Babylonian idol gods.

Paul encourages us to keep God's holy days. Many years after the crucifixion, he said he had to keep them. If God had abolished them, Paul would have known about it (John 14:26): *But bade them farewell, saying, I must by all means keep this feast . . .* (Acts 18:21). *Therefore let us keep the feast . . .* (1 Cor. 5:8).

He says he must by all means keep the feast, not because he feels like it or thinks maybe he should from the goodness of his heart. He says *I must* and *by all means*, and not because of the Jews. Is there any indication that he is doing it because of a tradition or because of respect for any persons or religion?—Absolutely not. He is doing it for the same reason that he says in his testimonies; he is doing it for the Messiah, as He revealed it to him.

Just for a point of interest, stats show that North American retail stores earn on average well over half of their annual profit around these holidays. No wonder January has more depression related illnesses than the rest of the year combined. Much of the depression is debt-related. Society at large has accepted the fact that it is normal to rack up debt, like on high interest credit cards, for the festive seasons; especially Christmas. For many bread-winners it will take a few months to pay off that debt. On top of that, Christmas happens to be in the gloomy time of year, especially up North where there is very little sunshine during the mid-winter months.

5c. Paul's Doctrines

The Messiah promised His disciples that God would send them the Holy Spirit to guide them and remind them of everything that He had taught them: *But the Comforter, which is the Holy Ghost, whom the Father will send in my name, he shall teach you all things, and bring all things to your remembrance, whatsoever I have said unto you* (John 14:26). Accordingly, if any laws had changed, like the Lord's Sabbaths (weekly and annual), or His food laws, the apostles would have known it firsthand. We need to believe what the Messiah said here.

> *But I certify you, brethren, that the gospel which was preached of me is **not after man**. For I neither received it of man, neither was I taught it, but by the revelation of Jesus Christ* (Gal. 1:11-12). *Be ye followers of me, even as I also am of Christ. Now I praise you, brethren, that ye remember me in all things, and keep the ordinances* <paradosis>,[14] *as I delivered them to you* (1 Cor. 11:1–2).

Paul commands us to keep the ordinances (precepts) as he delivered them to us, which was as the Lord revealed them to him.

I hear traditional Christians and their preachers say that Paul and the Messiah did many of the things they did, like keeping God's holy days and His Sabbaths (the weekly and annual Sabbaths), to keep peace with the Jews. This is absolutely ludicrous because Paul makes it so clear throughout his epistles that we are to follow his doctrines, as the Messiah delivered them through him. When I speak against keeping traditions as doctrines, I've had Scriptures thrown in my face like, *Submit yourselves to every ordinance* **<ktisis>**[15] *of man for the Lord's sake . . .* (1 Peter 2:13). When we study the words, we see that the word *ordinance* in 1 Corinthians 11:2 was translated from the Greek word <paradosis>, [14] which means *concretely a precept.* In 1 Peter 2:13, they used the word *ordinance* to translate the Greek word <ktisis>, [15] which means *a creation; somebody, or something created.* Peter is commanding us to not be rebellious to the rulers and masters, because they are also God's creation, and He wants us to show them peace and respect. This agrees with what Paul had to say on that subject in Romans 13:1-10. And Peter, together with other apostles, commanded that we ought to obey the rulers and governors as long as it does not go against God's commands:

> *Saying, Did not we straitly command you that ye should not teach in this name? and, behold, ye have filled Jerusalem with your doctrine, and intend to bring this man's blood upon us. Then Peter and the other apostles answered and said, We ought to obey God rather than men* (Acts 5:28–29).

After reading a few accounts, as we did in Mark 7 and 2 Corinthians 6 and 11, does it sound as if there is any possibility that the Messiah and His apostles would observe any part of the traditional doctrines or ceremonies for the Jews? I think not. Consider this: While the Messiah was on this earth, before the crucifixion, the Old Testament

Jewish laws (as God's commandments are labeled by the preachers of this lie) were still binding on the people or, for argument's sake, at least to the Jews. Now, if our Lord and Savior, who was born a Jew, broke just one jot or tittle of God's food laws or His commandments; He disqualified Himself to be our saving Messiah, because to be the true Messiah He had to be absolutely and totally sinless and blameless (Isa. 53:9; Heb 4:15; Luke 23:41; 2 Cor. 5:21; 1 Peter 2:22; 1 John 3:5). On the contrary, the Messiah excoriated, and even condemned, the Pharisees for keeping the traditions of men. If we really believe that the Messiah observed man-made commandments <entalma>[11], or the Judaized version of God's commandments <entole>[7], we're making Him out to be a hypocrite. If you've been deceived by this lie, I advise you to think about it very hard and soberly, with an open and unbiased heart, because the teachers of such doctrines are preaching another messiah (2 Cor. 11:4; 1 Tim. 4:1–2).

> *I marvel that ye are so soon removed from him that called you into the grace of Christ unto another gospel: Which is not another; but there be some that trouble you, and would pervert the gospel of Christ.* **But though we, or an angel from heaven, preach any other gospel unto you than that which we have preached unto you, let him be accursed.** *As we said before, so say I now again, if any man preach any other gospel unto you than that ye have received, let him be accursed* (Gal. 1:6–9).

Paul is very sincere, bold, and sure that what he preached to them was directly from the Lawgiver and Messiah. He says that even if an angel from heaven were to come and preach anything other than that which He had preached to them before, that they were to curse them. If Paul had preached anything other than directly God's Word, he would have been accursed. He was, in essence, challenging angels from heaven to prove him. This is very sobering. He mentioned it to the Galatians when he was with them earlier, and he is mentioning it twice in this letter, to make absolutely certain that they would not need to doubt as to what he had said and whether he meant it.

Does this charge sound as if it is coming from someone who would consider teaching any sort or type of doctrine or tradition of men? Certainly not. And as we know, Paul was executed for his steadfastness in the faith that he held in the Messiah's sacrifice, for obeying His commandments <entole>[7], and for not obeying their (men's) commandments <entalma>[11]. If the Messiah and His apostles had followed after and taught men's traditions and doctrines and if they had not kept God's commandments, the world would not have needed to persecute them unto death.

Paul said that he taught only what was revealed to him by the Messiah. And the Messiah said that He kept God's commandments (John 15:10), and did only as His Father had taught Him: *I do nothing of myself; but as my Father hath taught me, I speak these things* (John 8:28). Let's consider this statement, which He made right in the middle of a vicious argument between Him and the Pharisees regarding His qualifications as king and Messiah (John 5–10). Sixteen verses later, He straightly tells them that they are of their father, the Devil. For what?—For perverting the laws and writings of Moses, which they swore to be living by; but were not (John 7:19). He said if they really believed Moses, they would know Him: *For had ye believed Moses, ye would have believed me: for he wrote of me. But if ye believe not his writings, how shall ye believe my words?* (John 5:46–47). But since they had perverted the Scriptures, it was impossible for them to believe Him, let alone know Him. Their traditions got in the way of God's

Holy Scriptures, wherefore they could not believe the truth. Such statements debunk and destroy, once for all, any and all beliefs that the Messiah or Paul would teach, or follow any doctrine other than that only from God.

Therefore, Paul's teachings are holy and God-breathed, as also are the epistles of the other apostles, and the rest of the Holy Scriptures (2 Peter 1;21). Paul is very serious and concerned about the Galatian people going either back to where they came from, to heathenism-paganism, and/ or to the syncretized Pharisaic traditional religion, which is Judaism. Neither of these religions have any means of justification from sin, wherefore they could lead only to eternal death, because both of those systems are leaving out the need for the Messiah's sacrifice.

We need to study the Scriptures and find out if the doctrines, traditions, holidays, and Sundays that we are observing and keeping holy have scriptural backup and authority. Do not just take this from me, or any carnal being. That is very dangerous. Don't get me wrong. I am not saying that you shouldn't listen to other people. What I mean is that your salvation has too high a price tag to not check it out for yourself in the Holy Scriptures. Do not rest the precious salvation of you and your family on another man's word, but only God's Word. So please let this type of information at least provoke you to examine it, and study and prove it from the Scriptures, for your own and your family's spiritual safety (1 Thess. 5:21; 2 Tim. 2:15). And then allow God to reveal His truth to you, which He will if you let Him. We must ask God through His Son, in prayer, unbiased, and with an open mind, ready to accept and make the changes when He reveals them, submissively and humbly, and He will give us wisdom and answer our prayers in His will and time: *If ye shall ask any thing in my name, I will do it* (John 14:14; read also James 1:5–6; 1 John 3:22).

5d. False Apostles

For many shall come in my name, saying, **I am Christ***; and shall deceive many* (Matt. 24:5). *And many false prophets shall rise, and shall deceive many. And because iniquity shall abound, the love of many shall wax cold* (Matt. 24:11–12). Notice He says they will say that *He*, the Lord, is the Messiah, not that *they* are. These lawless prophet preachers will profess that the Lord is the Messiah to make you and me believe that they are teaching the Messiah of the Holy Scriptures while actually preaching a demonized messiah who destroyed God's Commandments, thus using His name to deceive people with. This can come only from people who don't know Him, but know only *about* Him. It is in the traditional church system that the "law-done-away" doctrine is preached, not in or by the world. This is using the Lord's name in vain, thus breaking the third commandment—that is, of course, if you believe in God's commandments.

We are frequently warned to guard against the intrusion of false preachers: *Beware of false prophets, which come to you in sheep's clothing, but inwardly they are ravening wolves* (Matt. 7:15; read also 1 Peter 5:8). *Beloved, believe not every spirit, but try the spirits whether they are of God: because many false prophets are gone out into the world* (1 John 4:1). How can we try the spirits? It's not that hard to discern. Paul says the laws are spiritual (Romans 7:14). He says that the carnal mind hates God because of its inability to obey His laws while in that carnal state: *Because the carnal mind is enmity against God: for it is not subject to the law of God, neither indeed can be. So then they that are in the flesh cannot please God* (Rom. 8:7–8). We obviously need to be in the opposite state of mind to be able to become subjected to the law of God, which according to Paul, is required to be able to please God. What is the opposite of such a state? He says if God's Spirit is in us (Rom. 8:9–11), the mind will think spiritually (Rom. 8:4–5). According to these Scriptures, the mind has at this point become submissive to His laws. If we say that we have God's Spirit in us, but are not keeping His commandments, John says we're fibbing. He already gave us the answer, just before he commanded us to try the Spirit: *And hereby we do know that we know him, if we keep his commandments. He that saith, I know him, and keepeth not his commandments, is a liar, and the truth is not in him* (1 John 2:3–4). According to these Scriptures, if a person is not practicing the commandments of God, all ten of them, one cannot be from the God of heaven and earth. God is not the author of confusion (1 Cor. 14:33), and He makes His truth easy to understand for those who search Him as a child (Matt. 11:25).

Paul is constantly beating up on man-made traditions: *Beware lest any man spoil you through philosophy and vain deceit, after the tradition of men, after the rudiments of the world, and not after Christ* (Col. 2:8). *Let no man deceive you by any means...* (2 Thess. 2:3; cf. Matt. 24:4; Eph. 5:6).

Peter warns us how people will twist the Scriptures to fit their lawless doctrines:

> *And account that the longsuffering of our Lord is salvation; even as our beloved brother Paul also according to the wisdom given unto him hath written unto you; As also in* **all** *his epistles, speaking in them of these things; in which are some things hard to be understood, which they that are unlearned and unstable wrest, as they do also the other scriptures, unto their own destruction. Ye therefore, beloved, seeing ye know these things before, beware lest ye also, being led away with the error of the wicked* <**athesmos**>,[16] *fall from your own stedfastness* (2 Peter 3:15–17).

We ought to thank our merciful God for inspiring the apostles to warn us about such an important matter.

We have already learned a few points of what Peter is giving warning for, as we've gone over in the beginning of this section, namely, the manner in which Paul used the terms *laws, circumcision,* and *commandments* in his letters, and how the false preachers twist and pervert Scriptures to suit the doctrines of their church. Peter specifically states that such people twist Paul's Scriptures and also other Scriptures. It's quite logical, because if they twist any portion of any Scripture, they must twist also other Scriptures, not to eliminate but to reduce the weight of the contradictions that they have now created. And since such contradictions cannot be eliminated, they must confuse the Scriptures to a point where one must rely *solely* on their interpretation of the Scriptures to be able to make at least some sense of it. And as such, Scriptures become complicated and confusing (Babylonianized), with inevitable contradictions.

Paul tells us exactly how Satan will devise lustful, ear-itching doctrines to accomplish that mission: *For the time will come when they will not endure sound doctrine; but after their own lusts shall they heap to themselves teachers, having itching ears; And they shall turn away their ears from the truth, and shall be turned unto fables* (2 Tim. 4:3–4)—just as John put it in 1 John 2:3-4 (above). Jude warns us that they are in the churches: *For there are certain men crept in unawares, who were before of old ordained to this condemnation, ungodly men, turning the grace of our God into lasciviousness, and denying the only Lord God, and our Lord Jesus Christ* (Jude 4). People make permission through God's grace to lust after the world (lawlessness).

Wicked powers come through the *high places* (the pulpits?): *For we wrestle not against flesh and blood, but against principalities, against powers, against the rulers of the darkness of this world, against spiritual wickedness in high places* (Eph. 6:12). He explains who these rulers are:

For such are false apostles, deceitful workers, transforming themselves into the apostles of Christ. And no marvel; for Satan himself is transformed into an angel of light. Therefore it is no great thing if his ministers [preachers] *also be transformed as the ministers of righteousness; whose end shall be according to their works* (2 Cor. 11:13–15).

Read Jeremiah 23, 34, and 50, where God talks to just such ministers.

Angel of light, ministers of righteousness—it sends shivers down one's spine to think who these ministers might be. We can be certain that Paul had in mind every minister who does not use the absolute and only truth and instructions from God, which are in His moral and spiritual laws, the Ten Commandments. Anyone who teaches lawlessness cannot be of God, because God is the author of eternal law and order: *He that saith, I know him, and keepeth not his commandments, is a liar, and the truth is not in him* (1 John 2:4). And the Messiah condemned lawlessness: *Not every one that saith unto me, Lord, Lord, shall enter into the kingdom of heaven; but he that doeth the will of my Father which is in heaven. Many will say to me in that day, Lord, Lord, have we not prophesied in thy name? and in thy name have cast out devils? and in thy name done many wonderful works? And then will I profess unto them, I never knew you: depart from me, ye that work **iniquity** <anomia>*[10] (Matt. 7:21–23). Iniquity means lawlessness. Read also Matthew 22:36–40, where the Messiah explains the Great Commandment. The first tablet is the instructions on how to love God. The second tablet is the instructions on how to love your neighbor. We are to walk with God in all righteousness. Not keeping God's laws is breaking them, which is unrighteousness: *All unrighteousness is sin . . .* (1 John 5:17). *Sin is the transgression of the law* (1 John 3:4).

What fellowship hath righteousness with unrighteousness <anomia>?[10] (2 Cor. 6:14). *My tongue shall speak of thy word: for all thy commandments are righteousness* (Ps. 119:172).

These lawless preachers of which the Messiah speaks in Matthew 7:15–23 will do many miracles to snare people into their religion. And the spiritually weak people will swallow hook, line, and sinker to belong to such a system, because as far as they can tell those miracles alone are a proof to them that the preacher doing such miracles must be from God. But as Moses prophesied in Deuteronomy 12:28–13:11, God will allow such miracles to be performed by false prophets in order to test us to see if that will seduce us away from Him. This is a sure test to see if we love God with all our heart and keep His commandments. As John said in 1 John 4:1, we must test the spirit of such a prophet to see if he is from God. If he is keeping all of God's commandments, he is from God. If he is not keeping, *and teaching* all of God's commandments, he cannot be from God. This is the one simple fail-safe test which God gave His people to measure up prophets and preachers. In Matthew 7:21-23 the Messiah confirms the prophecy of Deuteronomy 12 and 13, by clearly stating that **lawless** ministers will have deceived many people by actually having done miracles and wonders, ***in HIS name!***

6. Study God's Scriptures and Prove All Things from It Because Ignorance is No Excuse

Paul commands us to study and prove all things from the Scriptures: *Study to shew thyself approved unto God, a workman that needeth not to be ashamed, rightly dividing the word of truth* (2 Tim. 2:15). *Prove all things; hold fast that which is good. Abstain from all appearance of evil* (1 Thess. 5:21–22).

God says that ignorance will be no excuse for you and your descendants: *My people are destroyed for lack of knowledge: because thou hast rejected knowledge, I will also reject thee, that thou shalt be no priest to me: seeing thou hast forgotten the law of thy God, I will also forget thy children* (Hos. 4:6). Paul says the same: *Walk not as other Gentiles walk, in the vanity of their mind, Having the understanding darkened, being alienated from the life of God through the ignorance that is in them, because of the blindness of their heart* (Eph. 4:17–18). God gave even the heathen knowledge in their heart about His laws (Deut. 30:11; 31:12; Isa. 56:1-6; Rom. 2:11-29). Everyone will be judged accordingly (Luke 12:47–48), to each his own

(Ezek. 18:20). Reasoning that one was taught lies by a friend, parent, or preacher will be no excuse.

Paul explains in 2 Corinthians 3:14–4:4 that, because of the beliefs in other gods (traditions of men), the truth of the prophecies will remain veiled. Just as the Messiah said to the Pharisees; if they had believed Moses, as they professed they were, but were not; they would have known Him (John 5:46–47; 7:19). Only after we understand the true purpose of the Messiah's sacrifice, such as what He did while He was on earth and what He didn't do, what He fulfilled, what He didn't fulfill, and what He will yet fulfill, will we be able to understand the prophecies of the Scripture. At that point it will reveal our sins, thus tormenting our pride:

> *But if our gospel be hid, it is hid to them that are lost: In whom the god of this world hath blinded the minds of them which believe not, lest the light of the glorious gospel of Christ, who is the image of God, should shine unto them* (2 Cor. 4:3–4; read also Isa. 28:13; Matt. 11:25; 13:10–15).

Ignorance is no excuse. This is the opposite of a traditional teaching that discourages us from studying the Scriptures, because they claim that the more you know, the more God will require of you. This has been taken out of context and is not the scriptural truth. God is just, and he will not punish you for what you honestly didn't know. But if you intentionally keep yourself ignorant for such a purpose, He will pour out His wrath the more; He is not mocked: *Be not deceived; God is not mocked: for whatsoever a man soweth, that shall he also reap.* (Gal. 6:7). God wants us to get to know Him, study Him, and learn His ways until we know enough about Him that we desire to be like Him, whereby we will learn to live and walk in His ways.

For our benefit, we need to prove all things from Scripture, as the Bereans did: *These were more noble than those in Thessalonica, in that they received the word with all readiness of mind, and searched the scriptures daily, whether those things were so* (Acts 17:11). The Bereans readily accepted Paul's preaching which they proved with Old Testament Scriptures to see if it aligned with the Word of God. If Paul's teaching from the New Testament era had been changed to any extent from the Old Testament teaching, the Bereans would have rejected him, as they had only the Old Testament scrolls to confirm it with.

7. God's Laws are Not Done Away

A common ear-tickling doctrine teaches that the commandments of God were nailed to the tree together with the same One who spoke them from Mount Sinai and inscribed them into stone tablets with His finger. About 1,500 years later this same One came to earth to practice them perfectly, whereby He magnified them: *The LORD is well pleased for his righteousness' sake; he will magnify the law, and make it honourable* (Isa. 42:21). This was the Messiah, our Lawmaker, Healer, and Redeemer, who commanded His followers to keep them, that is, if they really loved Him and wanted eternal life: *If ye love me, keep my commandments* (John 14:15). *If thou wilt enter into life, keep the commandments* (Matt. 19:17). He, together with His apostles, said just the opposite of what the "law-done-away" preachers say: *Wherefore the law is holy, and the commandment holy, and just, and good* (Rom. 7:12). Luke recorded that Paul lived by and kept the law: . . . *that thou thyself also walkest orderly, and keepest the law* (Acts 21:24). Paul himself professes it: *For not the hearers of the law are just before God, but the doers of the law shall be justified* (Rom. 2:13). His mind served the law of God, although his flesh desired the law of sin: *So then with the*

mind I myself serve the law of God; but with the flesh the law of sin (Rom. 7:25).

James says that we are to be doers to the extent that it becomes like a habit, or a natural act:

> *But be ye doers of the word, and not hearers only, deceiving your own selves. For if any be a hearer of the word, and not a doer, he is like unto a man beholding his natural face in a glass: For he beholdeth himself, and goeth his way, and straightway forgetteth what manner of man he was. But whoso looketh into the perfect law of liberty, and continueth therein, he being not a forgetful hearer, but a doer of the work, this man shall be blessed in his deed* (James 1:22–25). *If ye fulfil the royal law according to the scripture, Thou shalt love thy neighbour as thyself, ye do well* (James 2:8; read also Deut. 6).

He says that, by diligently and continually practicing the perfect and royal law of liberty, by which he clearly points to the Ten Commandments, the result will be that we will have love for the neighbor, which according to the Messiah is the whole teaching of the Torah, the law, and the prophets (Matt. 22:36–40). The apostles agree that God's laws and commandments are important and good. Paul says that the Messiah is the goal and purpose (end) of the law, not the destroyer of it: *For Christ is the **end** <telos>[17] of the law <nomos>[6] for righteousness to every one that believeth* (Rom. 10:4). He is saying that the Messiah is the ultimate prophetic purpose of the law for righteousness for those who believe that He was the Lamb of God sacrifice.

The keeping of God's commandments is what defines God, and His love and mercy for His creation. That's why not one jot or tittle is done away (Matt. 5:18–19; 19:17).

We need to practice the commandments in their entirety (James 2:10–12) if we want to have liberty. Those who say they know God, but do not keep His commandments are liars (1 John 2:4) and as such are sinning (1 John 3:4). Those who deny these sayings are sinning yet again by lying, and calling God a liar (1 John 1:8–10). Why would John have said these things six decades after the crucifixion if the laws had been done away? If they had been abolished, he would surely have known it (John 14:26). The Messiah states a definite time until which they will not be done away: *And it is easier for heaven and earth to pass, than one tittle of the law to fail.* (Luke 16:17; read also Matt. 5:17–19). Have heaven and earth passed? Has all been fulfilled? It requires only a small measure of wisdom to answer that; but it takes a religiously trained theologian to confuse it.

God tells us in very plain language who will have the wisdom to understand Him:

> *The fear of the LORD is the beginning of wisdom: a good understanding have all they that do his commandments . . .* (Ps. 111:10).
> *The law of the LORD is perfect, converting the soul: the testimony of the LORD is sure, making wise the simple. The statutes of the LORD are right, rejoicing the heart: the commandment of the LORD is pure, enlightening the eyes. The fear of the LORD is clean, enduring for ever: the judgments of the LORD are true and righteous altogether. More to be desired are they than gold, yea, than much fine gold: sweeter also than honey and the honeycomb. Moreover by them is thy servant warned: and in keeping of them there is great reward* (Ps. 19:7–11).

According to God's Word, those who practice His commandments will have understanding of Him. On the flipside, those who do not keep God's commandments will not understand Him. Do any of these Scriptures suggest that God's laws and commandments are burdensome or have been done away? Or that obeying them will hinder one's salvation? According to God's Word, obeying them delivers goodness and blessings, and disobeying them delivers curses and death. This is the exact opposite of what we hear from the "law-done-away" Christians, who claim that keeping God's commandments brings death by curses and not keeping them delivers salvation by grace.

I will give a scenario to show how the phrase *yoke of bondage* was used by Paul, and compare it with what the 'law-done-away' theologians and commentators have interpreted it to mean by perverting it in order to support their "law-done-away" philosophy. We will start off by defining what a yoke is and how it applies to our modern-day practices.

I trust that we already understand that *yoke of bondage* as used in the Scriptures always refers to the enslavement elements imposed by man-made traditions and doctrines, which usually come from the fathers and elders of religious systems, and as such are rudiments and elements of this Satan-ruled world. By using man's traditions as doctrines, God's commandments are inevitably forsaken, whereby the whole religion becomes burdensome, grievous, and hard to be borne, resulting in worthless and vain worship. This is the opposite of the liberty that God promises to those who accept and obey His laws and commandments as doctrines.

The Pharisees, because of their demon-driven traditions, did not accept the Lord as their saving Messiah, wherefore they could not understand the need of His sacrifice. Had they practiced God's commandments properly, as we just learned, they would have been given the wisdom to understand God and the Messiah. But since they used their doctrines as commandments, they received the honor and glory. This is how Satan's pride works in man. And by agreeing to follow that religion, one had to be circumcised as a sign that one was justified by that system, which glorified them. Thus one was yoked to that system.

This is similar to most of today's traditional churches. To become a member of a church, you agree to observe and obey the doctrines of that church. By agreeing to this system, you customarily get baptized (circumcised), into their belief system, whereby in most churches, you become justified by following the doctrines of that system. And as a faithful member, you are yoked to their system. There is nothing wrong with being yoked or committed to something as long as it does not commit you to something that would run contrary to God's laws. If the church with which you have become yoked observes man-made traditions and pagan practices, you are now yoked to their package of laws, whereby the plagues of Revelation 18:4 will inevitably befall you. Of course, the leaders of such system will tell you that all their doctrines are based upon the laws of God.

The new covenant comes with a yoke, just as did the old covenant and the Abrahamic covenant. It is an agreement to the terms and conditions of a contract. A bank loan also comes with a yoke, by which we are obligated to meet certain terms and conditions of a contract (covenant), which we have to sign, thereby choosing and promising to follow the terms and conditions of that agreement. The bank puts a yoke upon us, as according to their standards. Now we have to make payments that are technically called *a burden*. As long as we can make the payments, they are bearable, and as such there may be nothing wrong with that yoke. It commits us to our obligations of that contract. I'm not encouraging debt, but I'm using this analogy because most people will understand it.

But when we borrow more, it can get to a point where the burden becomes unbearable, at which time the bank will legally call that loan and take what is theirs, leaving us with potentially nothing. We might call this a type of death sentence to our business, because the terms (laws) of that contract (covenant) have claimed their dues, payment in full (bondage to sin and death, the curse of the law), which resulted in death to that business.

There are two ways to be freed from that death sentence. One is that we have paid it back in full, as per the agreement, whereby we become justified, set free from the penalty that would occur if we would not be able to make the payments, which would have been a transgression of the terms and conditions of that agreement or contract. The other way is that the bank would, while we still owe the money, give us back the contract marked "Paid in Full" or "Pardoned from This Debt" and signed by the bank owner, who is the justifier of that decision, undeserved and unearned. That's grace. Now we've been saved from the curse of that unpayable loan, by his grace, which reconciles us to the bank. This begs a few questions:

1. Since the banker, by his grace, saved us from that penalty, are the terms and conditions (laws) of the bank now abolished because we have been justified from that contract? I say no! The same terms and conditions will be used again if and when we borrow money again (become indebted).

2. Were the burdens that became unbearable, which brought on the death sentence, the fault of the lender (lawgiver)? Of course not. Just the same, transgressing God's laws, which automatically charges us with a penalty, is a voluntary act of ourselves, and not the fault of the Lawgiver, wherefore we can see that the burdens (indebtedness), whether in banking or from sinning, are self-inflicted. In the case of God's law, it can guide us, and transgressed it can only convict and condemn us (Rom. 7:7), in hopes that it will bring us unto repentance, whereby He will justify

(forgive) us of that sin, thus discharging the penalty by His grace.

I will use another example. Let's say we get fined by the law for driving through a stop sign. We agree that we are guilty and pay the fine to the judge of the court. Does that mean that the lawmaker will now permit us to ignore stop signs? This is very similar to how Jude put it in verse 4. Or would he perhaps now just simply abolish stop signs?

Or let's say we get pulled over and fined for driving 90 mph in a 60-mph zone. We agree that we are guilty and pay the fine to the judge. Or better yet, our dad, as a type of savior, because of his unconditional love for us, chooses, *by his grace*, to take our rap and pay the fine, which the judge accepts. Will the lawmaker now permit us to determine our own speed limit, or would he abolish the speed limit on the highway altogether? Of course not. Why then does the traditional Christian believe that God's laws are done away because the Messiah paid the penalty for our *past* transgression of them? (Rom. 3:25)

I realize these analogies are weak. But I hope it helps to understand that, just the same, God's commandments will convict us time and again, whenever we unwillingly break them, whereby we become indebted to the Messiah's blood, which brings a sentence upon us. Repenting of it, and being forgiven (justified), does not do away with the laws that we transgressed.

When we get baptized by the Holy Spirit we agree, or get yoked, to observe and obey the commandments of our God and Creator of heaven and earth, and none other. We know now that there is no room for any pagan traditions and doctrines. We have no more excuse for not knowing.

Do we realize what we are doing by observing the pagan traditions of mankind, which come from the gods of this world? Do we ever stop to think what we agreed to when we signed on to the Holy Spirit, literally yoked ourselves to the Messiah's commandments through His shed blood? Did we count the cost of turning away from paganism and the pleasures of this world when we chose to repent of them and turn to Him and Him alone? (Luke 14).

In some Bible margins and commentaries, theologians have related Galatians 5:1 to Acts 15:10 and then to Matthew 23:4 because of the word *yoke* and phrases like *binding heavy burdens* being used in these Scriptures. They perversely reference these phrases and connect them together in a way to try to make them say that obeying God's laws and commandments and observing His holy days are unbearably burdensome. These references have been put there by typical modern-day theologians who obviously had a "law-done-away" mindset. And they have done this in an effort to support that "law-done-away" doctrine. So they try to make a more binding conclusion by persuading the readers that the Messiah and His apostles were referring to God's commandments as being burdensome, grievous, unbearable, and eventually condemned by the Messiah. I will do a brief review of these Scriptures to show how they have perverted them to support their traditional doctrines.

I will start with a heads-up on a few general terms that we learned earlier. We know what Paul means by *yoke of bondage* and his usual use of the terms *law of Moses* and *circumcision*. We know that the Messiah calls His yoke easy and His burden light. And we know that man-made traditions are burdensome and that God's laws are liberty.

I will start with Galatians 5:1: *Stand fast therefore in the liberty wherewith Christ hath made us free, and be not entangled again with the **yoke of bondage**.* As we learned in section 5, Paul excoriated the people of Galatia for observing days and months and times and years while they were yet serving the gods that were not gods by nature (Gal. 4:8–10). This ought to give us a strong clue as to what he referred to by *yoke of bondage* here. There is no doubt that there were Pharisees in Galatia at that time who had infiltrated the beliefs of these Galatian Gentiles with many of their Judaized and perverted doctrines and commandments, and vice versa. We can ascertain that Paul was referring to the Judaized doctrines as well as the Gentile doctrines, which are all unable to justify a man from sin, which makes them burdensome, worthless, and vain. That is the yoke of bondage. We can know with certainty that the bondage that Paul referred to in Galatians is not bearing on God's commandments but on man's. The fact that this account involves strict commandment <entalma>[11] keeping Jews, does not make any allowance to label God's laws and commandments <entole>[7] as burdensome or a yoke of bondage. But that is what we see them do in many commentaries, after which it is preached. Remember from Mark 7 that the Pharisees were not keeping God's commandments but their Judaized version of them, which was vain. Nor were they keeping the laws of Moses (John 7:19).

So the traditional Christians take *yoke of bondage* from Galatians 5:1 and connect it to Acts 15:10 because of the similar wording, *yoke upon the neck* and *not able to bear: Now therefore why tempt ye God, to put a **yoke upon the neck** of the disciples, which neither our fathers **nor we were able to bear?** (Acts 15:10). Peter speaks of an unbearable yoke. He is clearly referring to the argument that the Pharisees presented in verse 5, whether the Gentiles in question should be circumcised and keep the law of Moses: But there rose up certain of the sect of the Pharisees which believed, saying, That it was needful to **circumcise** them, and to command them to keep the **law of Moses** (Acts 15:5). This would most assuredly include the whole Pharisaic package of laws, which Peter was well aware of: Forasmuch as ye know that ye were not redeemed with corruptible things, as silver and gold, from your **vain conversation received by tradition from your fathers** (1 Peter 1:18).

Next they connect it to Matthew 23:4, for the same purpose of similar word usage, something *burdensome and unbearable: For they bind **heavy burdens** and **grievous** to be borne, and lay them on men's shoulders; but they themselves will not move them with one of their fingers. But all their works they do for **to be seen of men** . . .* (Matt. 23:4–5). Considering the context, each of these three Scriptures refers to a very burdensome yoke.

You need to read Matthew 23 before continuing. You will see that the pride in the hearts of the scribes and Pharisees caused them to pervert God's laws in a way that made it extremely grievous for their followers. The issue is pride. You will see how the Messiah flat-out condemns the glory-seeking and control-mongering Pharisees for hypocritically burdening the people with those unbearable duties solely for their gain. Although they were teaching about the laws and commandments of God, it was their corrupting of them by their traditions that made them grievous and unbearable. You will see that it removes many a contradiction when reading the Holy Scriptures after acknowledging this truth.

Peter would never say that keeping God's laws and commandments was unbearable. But he knew that the Pharisaic package of laws was totally unbearable. Everything that God ever commanded of His people was always for the betterment and liberation of mankind. That's why James still called them the perfect and royal laws of liberty (James 1:25; 2:8, 12) decades after the crucifixion. After all, God promises that He will never allow us to be tempted with more than we can bear:

> *There hath no temptation taken you but such as is common to man: but God is faithful, who will not suffer you to be tempted above that ye are able; but will with the temptation also make a way to escape, that ye may be able*

to bear it. Wherefore, my dearly beloved, flee from idolatry (1 Cor. 10:13–14).

Idolatry is adultery to God, which was, and still is, the main cause of people failing God. When we take part in anything that is of pagan origin, we commit idolatry and adultery with God. He calls it flirting or whoring with foreign gods: *And they transgressed against the God of their fathers, and went a **whoring** after the **gods of the people** of the land, whom God destroyed before them* (1 Chron. 5:25; read also Jer. 3; 1 Cor. 3:17; 10:1-21).

I trust that we now have an understanding of the fact that, when the Messiah and His apostles spoke about burdensome commandments, they always referred to the man-made traditions. Such traditions usually come from the fathers and elders and are passed on from generation to generation and preached to their followers as doctrines and commandments of God. Such were the traditions that the Pharisees got condemned for in Matthew 15 and 23, Mark 7, and John 5–10. The Scriptures all agree on that point without any contradictions whatsoever.

And finally, our Messiah makes us an offer to take His yoke upon us which is easy, and a burden which is light (Matt. 11:28–30). For those Christians who claim that God's laws and commandments of the Old Testament times were a burdensome yoke of bondage, the Messiah made this offer while they were still under the animal sacrificial and ritualistic laws. According to His Word, even doing all those sacrifices and rituals were an easy yoke and a light burden. His yoke is a commitment to continually (daily) follow after Him, according to His royal laws of liberty, which will keep (guard) one from the burdens of man's laws: *And he said to them all, If any man will come after me, let him deny himself, and take up his cross **daily**, and follow me* (Luke 9:23). The Messiah gave the following instructions:

If ye love me, keep my commandments (John
14:15). *If thou wilt enter into life, keep the
commandments* (Matt. 19:17). *If ye keep my
commandments, ye shall abide in my love; even
as I have kept my Father's commandments,
and abide in his love* (John 15:10). *And why
call ye me, Lord, Lord, and do not the things
which I say* (Luke 6:46)?

John understood the Messiah: *He that saith he abideth in
him ought himself also so to walk, even as he walked* (1 John
2:6). The Messiah's yoke is His instruction on how to attain
the <agape>[1] love and mercy of God, which can come only
from keeping the commandments of God and not man.
And as we have seen, because of the perverting of certain
Scriptures by the church fathers of old, the traditional
church system has been established upon a foundation
that has tragically labeled God's commandments a yoke of
bondage.

The message of the Messiah and His apostles all point to
the fact that the traditional doctrines of man are grievous,
burdensome, and unbearable, and that the doctrines that
are grounded in the laws and commandments of God are
easy and light. That is so because the Holy Spirit can be of
help only when we follow God's instructions, His laws and
commandments, whereby we will have the <agape>[1] love
and mercy of God dwelling in our heart. And such a heart
will always desire to do to a neighbor only such things
from which the neighbor would benefit (Luke 6:31; Rom.
13:10).

The Pharisees were always looking for ways to find
glory for themselves, of course through oppressing other
people, at the expense of the Messiah's shed blood. And
since they did not accept the Lord as their Messiah, their
concept of circumcision became so much more important
to them, as it was their proof that they were being glorified

by the people whom they persuaded to be justified by their traditional religious standards. That is the very reason why Paul harps so heavy on circumcision. When he talked about this Pharisaic Judaized system as laws or circumcision, the people of that time knew what he meant. In some instances, he called Gentiles *uncircumcision* because they were not circumcised (not certified) to that system. And he called the Jews *circumcision* because they were circumcised (certified) to that system: *For neither they themselves who are circumcised keep the law; but desire to have you circumcised, that they may glory in your flesh.* (Gal. 6:13; read also Rom. 2:28–29; Phil. 3:3). This verse proves how they loved to be glorified and that the laws they were keeping were not God's laws. We can be certain that Paul is not referring to obedience to God's commandments when he talks about the yoke of bondage in Galatians, and he is not doing away with any of God's laws.

8. Justified by Faith, through Love

Paul explains that the ingredients of circumcision and uncircumcision, by all of its Judaized definitions, are irrelevant to having the righteousness of the Messiah imputed to us. Of course the Pharisees could not see any other way to be justified than by literal circumcision and by keeping the sacrificial and ritual laws. They believed that being the fleshly descendants of Abraham, coupled with the literal circumcision of the flesh, was the only way to be justified before God. It is important to note that God never justified anyone by those standards. But through this Judaized doctrine, they were convinced that they had no sin, because they were descendants of Abraham and were circumcised in the flesh. If you bear this in mind while reading John 5–10, you will see that the violent argument that these Pharisees had with the Messiah concerning His Messiahship hinged on that very fact.

As a topic of faith and justification, which we have already addressed, this was the battle that Paul had in most, if not all, of the communities where he went to preach the gospel of the Messiah and the great news of the coming kingdom of God. The glory-seeking and control-mongering pride of the Pharisees was jeopardized whenever the gospel was preached to the extent that the Messiah had, as the sacrificial Lamb of God, fulfilled the animal sacrificial and ritualistic laws. Paul says that we will not be justified by doing those things, because we can only be justified by God's grace, through our faith in the blood of the sacrifice of the Messiah. He knew, as the Messiah said, that we must start by seeking out God's kingdom: *Seek ye first the kingdom of God, and His righteousness; and all these things shall be added unto you* (Matt. 6:33). By seeking out the purpose of His coming kingdom, we will develop a strong desire to become a part of it, thereby building up our faith in the Messiah's sacrifice, without which we cannot have any part in it.

That faith, as Paul preached it, comes through love, not by prescribing to the Judaized description of circumcision. The animal sacrifices were a foreshadow of the true Lamb of God that was to come, the Messiah (the Anointed One), who would lay down His life for all mankind. And He did come and, through His <agape>[1] love for us, did sacrifice His life (John 3:16; 1 John 3:16) in order to redeem us from the penalty of our past transgressions (Rom. 3:25). And if we believe this from our heart, which requires His faith, it will develop in us that same love for our brethren, whereby we will tear free from the world and become an acceptable sacrifice for Him (Rom. 12:1–2; James 4:4). Simply put, the Father's love in our heart will establish our faith in the sacrifice of the Messiah. *For in Jesus Christ neither circumcision availeth any thing, nor uncircumcision; but faith which worketh by love* <agape>[1] (Gal. 5:6). As faith works by and through the Father's love in our heart, it is the seed of the new creature to be conformed into the image of the Messiah (Rom. 8:29), which is the last Adam (1 Cor. 15:45–47). *For in Christ Jesus neither circumcision availeth any thing, nor uncircumcision, but a new creature* (Gal. 6:15). The seed of the new creature is imparted to us by the baptism of the Holy Spirit, which is the love of God shed abroad in our heart (Rom. 5:5) by the Father through faith in the Messiah. For this seed to take root, we must die to the lusts and pleasures of the flesh, and of this world daily: repent and turn to God, and seek God's <agape>¹ love and His kingdom, whereby love for others will become the natural fruit of the new creature:

> *In Christ Jesus our Lord, I die daily* (1 Cor. 15:31; read also Rom. 8:36). *I beseech you therefore, brethren, by the mercies of God, that ye present your bodies a living sacrifice, holy, acceptable unto God, which is your reasonable service. And be not conformed to this world: but be ye transformed by the renewing of your mind, that ye may prove what is that good, and acceptable, and perfect, will of God* (Rom. 12:1–2; read also 1 Peter 2:5).

The constant giving up of one's self is the living sacrifice, which can come only from keeping the laws and commandments of God, which teach us about His love and mercy for all mankind, while guarding us through life's walk. That's why Paul reinforces keeping God's commandments: *Circumcision is nothing, and uncircumcision is nothing, but the **keeping of the commandments** <entole>⁷ of God* (1 Cor. 7:19).

According to Protestant doctrine, Paul just contradicted himself tremendously because they say that "Paul says everywhere that we are not to keep the laws and commandments of God." Does he contradict himself? Absolutely not. As we've seen, all the Scriptures support and complement each other, just as our Savior promised that they would: *The Scripture cannot be broken* (John 10:35).

When we study the Scriptures with a law-abiding mindset, they align perfectly, with not the slightest hint of any contradiction whatsoever. They are what we call justified in typing and computer language. When we align our script with the edges of the paper, we call that justified, in alignment and in harmony with what was intended. And once it is justified by the edge of the paper, it does not do away with what it was justified by. The edge of the paper is still there, without which justification is not required.

The keeping of God's commandments is the <agape>[1] love of God, which produces our faith in the Messiah's sacrifice, wherefore He imputes the Savior's righteousness to us, by His grace.

9. Of Faith and Works

We've been taught by traditional church doctrines that practicing God's commandments is trying to earn one's salvation; they call it *the works of the law*. I have a few questions for the believers of this concept: What kind of work is required to bow down to the God of heaven and earth? How much work is needed to not bow down to Baal's ceremonies and trappings? What kind of work is required to rest and keep the LORD's Sabbath day holy, which our Creator God of heaven and earth sanctified to be kept holy for Him? How does it stack up against whatever is required to keep a day for the sun god? How much work is needed to honor your father and mother; to not commit adultery with the neighbor's wife or husband; to not lie, cheat, and steal; or to not to covet what the neighbor has? How much work is it to not kill (or hate) another person? Please give at least yourself an honest answer before calling obedience to them *works* by which one might try to earn one's salvation.

For those who claim that the Old Testament is just a history book with stories of irrelevant and obsolete prophecies, there is ample evidence in the New Testament that proof is required to show that we have faith in the right God, the God of Abraham, Isaac, and Jacob; the God of Israel. And the testimonies in the New Testament confirm the validity of the prophecies of the Old Testament which are already fulfilled, and the ones yet to be fulfilled.

> *By faith Abraham, when he was tried, offered up Isaac: and he that had received the promises offered up his only begotten son, Of whom it was said, That in Isaac shall thy seed be called: Accounting that God was able to raise him up, even from the dead; from whence also he received him in a figure* (Heb. 11:17–19; read also Gen. 22).

James confirms the true proof of whether or not we have faith:

> *What doth it profit, my brethren, though a man say he hath faith, and have not works? can faith save him? If a brother or sister be naked, and destitute of daily food, And one of you say unto them, Depart in peace, be ye warmed and filled; notwithstanding ye give them not those things which are needful to the body; what doth it profit? Even so **faith, if it hath not works, is dead, being alone**. Yea, a man may say, Thou hast faith, and I have works: shew me thy faith without thy works, and I will shew thee my faith by my works. Thou believest that there is one God; thou doest well: the devils also believe, and tremble. But wilt thou know, O vain man, that faith without works is dead? Was not Abraham our father justified by works, when he had offered Isaac his son upon the altar? Seest thou how faith wrought with his works, and **by works was faith made perfect**? And the scripture was fulfilled which saith, Abraham*

*believed God, and it was imputed unto him for righteousness: and he was called the Friend of God. Ye see then how that **by works a man is justified, and not by faith only** (James 2:14–24).*

John had compassion for other people:

*Hereby perceive we the love of God, because he laid down his life for us: and we ought to **lay down our lives** for the brethren. But whoso hath this world's good, and seeth his brother have need, and shutteth up his bowels of compassion from him, how dwelleth the love of God in him? My little children, let us not love in word, neither in tongue; **but in deed and in truth** (1 John 3:16–18).*

The Protestants say that in the days of Moses they were saved by the works of the laws but that now we are saved by grace and grace alone. That is a lie from Satan, the Devil, who has deceived the whole world (Rev. 12:9). Nobody has ever been saved by the works of the laws, and no one ever will be. The apostle Paul, who apparently commanded this, confirms that it never was that way: *And by him all that believe are justified from all things, from which ye **could not be justified by the law of Moses** (Acts 13:39). God has always saved people only by His grace, through our faith in the Messiah, and there never has been any other way. In the days of old, the people who had faith in the promised Messiah to come were saved through faith, by God's grace, the same faith in the Messiah, who is now manifested, in Him who has been crucified, resurrected, and ascended into heaven and sits at the right hand of God the Father. I suggest that you read and study Hebrews 11 and James 2, where faith, and the works of it, is explained in wonderful and abundant detail. And there is no hint of this type of faith having anything to do with earning one's salvation. Instead, it will produce fruit to the effect that it will show to the world which God you fear, obey, and serve. Surely, this will make one a peculiar person. But that is what the God of Abraham said His people would be:

> *And the LORD hath avouched thee this day to be his **peculiar** people, as he hath promised thee, and that thou shouldest keep all his commandments* (Deut. 26:18). The God who does not change said this: *Who gave himself for us, that he might redeem us from all iniquity, and purify unto himself a **peculiar** people, zealous of good works* (Titus 2:14; read also 1 Peter 2:9; Rev.1:6; 5:10).

Throughout Scripture, it is made abundantly clear that nobody ever was justified by the sacrificial laws. That doesn't mean that the people before the crucifixion could not have their sins forgiven. If they repented (turned away from their sins and turned to God), He justified them (forgave them their sins), by His grace, through their faith and trust in Him.

> *If my people, which are called by my name, shall humble themselves, and pray, and seek my face, and turn from their wicked ways; then will I hear from heaven, and will forgive their sin, and will heal their land* (2 Chron. 7:14). *But ye that did cleave unto the LORD your God are alive every one of you this day* (Deut. 4:4).

By God's grace, through their faith in Him, those called by His name were justified. Paul calls God's congregation the

Israel of God in Galatians 6:16. God's people are called by the same name throughout His Scriptures:

> *And I will dwell among the children of Israel, and will not forsake **my people Israel** (1 Kings 6:13). And thou Bethlehem, in the land of Juda, art not the least among the princes of Juda: for out of thee shall come a Governor, that shall rule **my people Israel** (Matt. 2:6).*

Martin Luther was a Roman Catholic priest with a doctor's degree in theology. At age thirty-four, his personal beliefs started conflicting with the Catholic system of indulgences and the papacy. He translated the Scriptures into German and started a new and reformed religion, after which he is known as the great Reformer. His motive was right, but he never severed from many of the pagan customs and traditions of the Holy Roman system. As the forerunner of the Protestant Reformation movement, those deep-rooted customs and traditions formed very weighty ingredients of the doctrinal foundation, of which today's traditional church system still remains a victim. As I briefly described in the inset at the end of section 5a, Luther was extremely anti-Jew, which caused him to hate Scriptures that encourage practicing the commandments of God. That's why Luther called the epistle of James a book of straw. James preached that our works would prove our faith and whose commandments we practice. James loved God's commandments and instructed us to keep them, which contradicts the traditional Lutheran-based grace-alone doctrines. I encourage you to read the book which Martin Luther wrote about his extreme hatred for the Jews *'The Jews and Their Lies'* which he wrote in 1545. Adolf Hitler used such information as a blueprint to justify what he did to the Jews in the Holocaust.

Because of this anti-Jew foundation of old, the traditional church system has negated the LORD's Sabbaths (the weekly Sabbaths and the annual Holy day Sabbaths). It seems as though they've adopted the anti-Jew mentality of perverted church fathers like Constantine and Luther into their church doctrinal system in a way to say that, whatever the Jews do, whether for the purpose of following their Pharisaic and Judaized doctrines or for the God of Abraham, their conclusion is absolute: if the Jews are doing it, it must be condemned and refrained from at all cost, especially if it's something that will reveal obedience to the commandments of the God of heaven and earth.

I will give you just a few examples of how Luther translated the Scriptures in a way to support those traditional beliefs. In Romans 3:28, he translated it to read *by faith alone.* He added the word *alone* to support the belief that if you practice the Ten Commandments, you are doing works, which is not of faith, and as such you have fallen from God's grace. Knowing where he came from, it's true to the extent that the pope's rituals can no more save a man than can the Pharisaic system. But he clearly went overboard in that area, while at the same time, he added and deleted words in other places to support certain pagan doctrines and philosophies that he had inherited from the Catholic system. These doctrines were engraved into his brain with which he couldn't part. He used the word *Easter* fifteen times in place of *Passover* in the New Testament and once in the Old Testament. Because that he took the liberty to add and remove words from the Scriptures is why he had no use for the book of Revelation, nor the Torah: *For I testify unto every man that heareth the words of the prophecy of this book, If any man shall **add** unto these things, God shall add unto him the plagues that are written in this book: And if any man shall **take away** from the words of the book of this prophecy, God shall take away his part out of the book of life, and out of the holy city, and from the things which are* *written in this book* (Rev. 22:18–19). *Ye shall not add unto the word which I command you, neither shall ye diminish ought from it, that ye may keep the commandments of the LORD your God which I command you.* (Deut. 4:2; read also 12:32).

As we know, Paul frequently used the words *law* <nomos>[6] and *circumcision* to point to the animal sacrificing and ritualistic part of the law. We learned at the end of section 8 that Paul specifically used the word <entole>[7] to point to the Ten Commandments. As we saw in section 7, Paul states in Romans 10:4 that the Messiah was the prophesied goal (end) <telos>[17] of the law for righteousness for those who believe that He is the sacrificial Lamb of God. Luther carefully chose the words and left out the words *for righteousness* in order to support his traditional belief that the laws and commandments of God as a whole were nailed to the tree together with the Messiah. By deleting the words *for righteousness*, the law loses its identity. And this is one of his greater apostasies, which Constantine, as a very influential emperor and church father, taught with extreme aggression, and passed it along.

It's quite obvious in Romans 9:30–10:5 that Paul was referring to the laws <nomos>[6] pertaining to the animal sacrifices and rituals that God specifically designed for the purpose of building up their faith in the sacrifice of the Messiah as the true Lamb of God, who would come to take away the penalty of their sins, by which they would be made righteous. This was the goal (end) <telos>[17] of these laws, as was foreshadowed in the law and prophecies of the Scriptures and specifically depicted in the ceremonial teachings of the animal sacrificial and ritualistic laws, which could not take the sins away but merely atoned (covered) them and reminded them of the need of a promised Savior who would take them away (Heb. 10:1–11). Faith in that promise was the righteousness of the law. How this law took the Israelites to that faith is Paul's emphasis in

Galatians 3. He often compares the righteousness of the laws, referred to as either the laws for righteousness or the laws of Moses, with the righteousness of the faith in the Messiah's sacrifice, referred to as the law of the Messiah. He refers to these laws <nomos>[6] as law for righteousness in Romans 10:4 to identify which aspect of the law he is referring to.

I'll show a few more Scriptures to confirm which aspects of the law Paul is referring to in Romans 10:4. They are the same works of the laws of Galatians 2:16 as we reviewed in section 5a:

> *But Israel, which followed after the law* <nomos>[6] *of righteousness, hath not attained to the law* <nomos>[6] *of righteousness. Wherefore? Because they sought it **not by faith**, but as it were by the works **<ergon>**[9] of the law* <nomos>.[6] *For they stumbled at that stumblingstone* (Rom. 9:31–32).

He's talking about laws that required physical labor. Sacrificing animals was a duty that required manual labor <ergon>[9] to be performed continually. God used His laws in many ways to guard and protect His children from the pagan customs and wicked habits of the heathen nations around them: *But before faith came, we were **kept** **<phroureo>**[18] under the law . . .* (Gal. 3:23). This was how He guarded them, and hemmed them in, to protect them from the wickedness of the pagan world around them. Keeping them busy would also help to accomplish that.

Paul commanded us to come out of this world and follow after the Messiah as a living sacrifice (Rom. 12:1–2). The Messiah preached that, if we want to follow Him, we must bear our cross daily, after His example (Luke 9:23). Paul said that he died to self daily (1 Cor. 15:31). The Messiah said not one jot or tittle would pass from the law

(Matt. 5:17–19). We can see that the duty of a committed follower of the Messiah will be just as busy, as a living sacrifice, as they were while they still sacrificed animals. And when the Messiah (the stumblingstone) laid down His life as the ultimate sacrifice, the self-righteousness of the Pharisees did not allow them to accept the righteousness of the saving Messiah. They had not kept the faith: *For unto us was the gospel preached, as well as unto them: but the word preached did not profit them, **not being mixed with faith** in them that heard it* (Heb. 4:2).

We have just gone over the main changes that occurred when the Messiah was crucified and resurrected, which were prophesied to occur. And there is yet much more to come. It is important to know about these changes, to understand the righteousness of the law of which the Scriptures speak, especially in Romans and Hebrews. Moses was the mediator of the law for righteousness of the old covenant, which pertained to the animal sacrifices, food and drink offerings, and ritualistic system, sometimes called the law of Moses. The Messiah is the mediator of the law for righteousness of the new covenant, which pertains to the sacrifice and offering of His life and blood for the redemption of our sins. Paul calls this the law of the Messiah: *Bear ye one another's burdens, and so fulfill the **law of Christ*** (Gal. 6:2). It takes <agape>[1] love to be able to bear another's burdens. And to obtain <agape>[1] love requires keeping God's commandments (1 John 5:2–3; 2 John 1:6).

If you will study Romans 9–12, you will see that Paul is explaining how God's plan was to strip everyone (Jews, other Israelites, and strangers) off His original (Israelitish) tree and root system in order that His grace could be given to all of mankind. Then He would graft all believers of the truth into that tree and root system. That truth is that the Messiah, as the unblemished Lamb of God, became our Passover: *Purge out therefore the old leaven, that ye may be a new lump, as ye are unleavened. For even* **Christ our passover is sacrificed for us** (1 Cor. 5:7). And as such, He fulfilled the animal sacrificial laws and rituals of the old covenant (Heb. 7–10). And this in no way made an end (abolishment) of God's eternal laws and commandments. There are about ten Greek words in the New Testament for which the KJV translators used the word 'end'. The word 'end' in Romans 10:4 is translated from the Greek word <telos>[17] meaning 'goal' and 'purpose'; and is used in the exact same sense in 1 Peter 1:9: *Receiving the end* <telos>[17] *of your faith . . .* Did Peter say that coming to the saving knowledge of the Messiah brought our faith to an *abolishing* end? Thankfully not! Therefore it is important to find the meaning of the Greek word to be able to understand the truth of that particular Scripture.

Just for information purposes, I will quote a couple of Scriptures that do use a word that indicates such an end, as an abolishment: *And it came to pass, when Jesus had made an* **end** <teleo>[19] *of commanding his twelve disciples, he departed thence to teach and to preach in their cities* (Matt. 11:1). *So shall it be at the end* **<sunteleia>**[20] *of the world: the angels shall come forth, and sever the wicked from among the just* (Matt. 13:49).

10. The Love of God

For God so loved the world, that he gave his only begotten Son, that whosoever believeth in him should not perish, but have everlasting life (John 3:16).

We'll find in the New Testament that the laws and commandments of God have existed since the beginning of time and that the keeping of them will produce the love of God in our hearts. As we've seen, they are not burdensome or a yoke of bondage:

> *And hereby we do know that we know him, if we keep his commandments* <entole>[7]. *He that saith, I know him, and keepeth not his commandments, is a liar, and the truth is not in him* (1 John 2:3–4). *Brethren, I write no new commandment unto you, but an old commandment which ye had from the beginning. The old commandment is the word which ye have heard from the beginning* (1 John 2:7).

Notice, he says *no new commandment*, but the same as was *from the beginning*, that is, God's moral laws of love and liberty, to love Him and the neighbor, quoted from the

Old Testament (Deut. 6:5; Lev. 19:17–18). We will receive blessings if we keep His commandments:

> *And whatsoever we ask, we receive of him, because we keep his commandments, and do those things that are pleasing in his sight. And this is his commandment, That we should believe on the name of his Son Jesus Christ, and love one another, as he gave us commandment. And he that keepeth his commandments dwelleth in him, and he in him. And hereby we know that he abideth in us, by the Spirit which he hath given* us (1 John 3:22–24). *He that loveth not knoweth not God; for* **God is love** <agape>[1] (1 John 4:8). *If a man say, I love God, and hateth his brother, he is a liar: for he that loveth not his brother whom he hath seen, how can he love God whom he hath not seen? And this commandment have we from him, That he who loveth God love his brother also* (1 John 4:20–21; John quoted this from Lev. 19:17–18). *By this we know that we love the children of God, when we love God, and keep his commandments. For this is the love of God, that we keep his commandments: and* **his commandments are not grievous** (1 John 5:2–3). *And this is love, that we walk after his commandments. This is the commandment, That, as ye have heard from the beginning, ye should walk in it* (2 John 1:6).

Wonderful harmony of the love of God. This is believing in the Messiah of John 3:16 and 1 John 3:16. Practicing the commandments as He instructs us to, not abolishing them, is our testimony that we do believe in Him. If this is doing works, then so be it. These are His instructions to us, and we must choose whom we will believe, and serve.

As our Savior says, *if thou wilt enter into life, keep the commandments* (Matt. 19:17). The Scriptures teach us how to show love first and utmost to God, and then also to the neighbor, which fulfills the law (Rom. 13:10; Gal. 6:2). We have seen in the Old and New Testament that one cannot love God unless one loves one's brother. (Deut. 6:5; Lev. 19:17–18; John 14:15; Rom. 13:8–10; Matt. 22:36–40; 1 John 4:20–21)

Please notice the seriousness of keeping God's commandments **and** of the faith in the Messiah. We can see why Satan is working so hard to deceive the whole world into believing that God's commandments are for the Jews and faith in the Messiah is for Christians. He has won perhaps billions of people by this one single doctrine alone. He has convinced the *Pharisaic* Jews of a false Messiah, just as he has convinced traditional Christianity of a lawless Messiah and that commandment-keeping is only for the Jews. Our living Savior has already defeated Satan who has nothing more to lose.

> *And the dragon was wroth with the woman, and went to make war with the remnant of her seed, which keep the commandments of God, **and** have the testimony of Jesus Christ* (Rev. 12:17). *Here is the patience of the saints: here are they that keep the commandments of God, **and** the faith of Jesus* (Rev. 14:12). Rev. 22:14 says: *Blessed are they that do his commandments, that they may have right to the **tree of life**, and may enter in through the gates into the city.*

This takes us right back to the garden of Eden. It has come full circle, without losing connection. Notice, God does not say the Jews who kept the commandments of God and the Christians who kept the faith of the Messiah, but those who kept both of those moral requirements were seen in the kingdom of God. I make notice of this for those who claim that God's commandments were for the Jews, and the faith of the Messiah is for Christians. As we have learned, there is no difference between Jew and Gentile, and He gave one law for all who believe in the God of Israel (Read 2 Chron. 19:7; Ex. 12:49; Num. 15:16; Mark 2:27–28; Rom. 2:11; Gal. 3:27–29).

For those that claim that God's Commandments didn't exist before Moses, or Mount Sinai; I will show some evidence from the New Testament, that they had to exist in the time of Adam. The sin of mankind entered the world through Adam, which brought about death (Rom 5:12-14). This occurred by transgressing God's law (1 John 3:4), for which the penalty was, and still is death (Gen.2:17; 3:3; and Rom. 6:23). Sin is not imputed where there is no law. Since death reigned through Adam's sin from Adam to Moses, God's laws had to be in existence already at that time in order to apply the death penalty to Adam and Eve and the following generations. The Scriptures do not clearly state when sin started, but Satan had already rebelled (sinned) toward God before he lied to Eve to tempt her to sin, who in turn enticed Adam to also sin. Thus their descendants sinned bad enough that God decided to drown the whole population (Gen.6:5-7), except righteous Noah and his immediate family. After the flood, sin and death still reigned, as to this day.

11. The Ten Commandments are Still in the Temple

And the temple of God was opened in heaven, and there was seen in his temple the ark of his [testament]: and there were lightnings, and voices, and thunderings, and an earthquake, and great hail (Rev. 11:19; the Greek Scripture says *covenant* instead of *testament*). These are the same events that took place when these testimonies came down from Mount Sinai:

> *And all the people saw the thunderings, and the lightnings, and the noise of the trumpet...* (Exod. 20:18). *And I turned myself and came down from the mount, and put the tables in the ark which I had made; and there they be, as the LORD commanded me.* (Deut. 10:5; read about this account in Exod. 19:16–20:22; Heb. 12:18–21).

John says in Revelation 11:19, the Ten Commandments are in the temple of God, just where God had Moses put them. Remember, Paul said in 2 Corinthians 6:16 and other Scriptures that we are the temple of the living God. So where are the laws, the Ten Commandments, now? As we will see, they are being trained into the faithful believers' hearts, God's temple, His new tabernacle and altar system. And God's altar has no place for paganism. (Read 1 Cor. 10:20–21; 2 Cor. 6:14–18.)

God's laws and commandments are eternal and for man's benefit. Typical traditional preachers imply that God made up His laws and commandments only to take pleasure in being harsh and cruel to His people. Moses didn't think so: *When thou art in tribulation, and all these things are come upon thee, **even in the latter days**, if thou turn to the LORD thy God, and shalt be obedient unto his voice; (For the LORD thy God is a merciful God;) he will not forsake thee, neither destroy thee, nor forget the covenant of thy fathers which he sware unto them. For ask now of the days that are past, which were before thee, since the day that God created man upon the earth, and ask from the one side of heaven unto the other, whether there hath been any such thing as this great thing is, or hath been heard like it? Did ever people hear the voice of God speaking out of the midst of the fire, as thou hast heard, and live? Or hath God assayed to go and take him a nation from the midst of another nation, by temptations, by signs, and by wonders, and by war, and by a mighty hand, and by a stretched out arm, and by great terrors, according to all that the LORD your God did for you in Egypt before your eyes? Unto thee it was shewed, that thou mightest know that the LORD he is God; there is none else beside him. Out of heaven he made thee to hear his voice, that he might instruct thee: and upon earth he shewed thee his great fire; and thou heardest his words out of the midst of the fire. And because he loved thy fathers, therefore he chose their seed after them, and brought thee out in his sight with his mighty power out of Egypt; To drive out nations from before thee greater and mightier than thou art, to bring thee in, to give thee their land for an inheritance, as it is this day. Know therefore this day, and consider it in thine heart, that the LORD he is God in heaven above, and upon the earth beneath: there* *is none else. Thou shalt keep therefore his statutes, and his commandments, which I command thee this day, that it may go well with thee, and with thy children after thee, and that thou mayest prolong thy days upon the earth, which the LORD thy God giveth thee, for ever* (Deut. 4:30–36; also read Ps. 119).

God does discipline-teach His people when they continually disobey His commandments. But He uses His laws to discipline them out of love in order to train them to be obedient to His ways: *For whom the Lord loveth he chasteneth* <**paideuo**>[21], *and scourgeth every son whom he receiveth. If ye endure chastening, God dealeth with you as with sons; for what son is he whom the father chasteneth not* (Heb. 12: 6–7)?

As God says through Moses, **in the latter days**, when tribulations come, make sure to keep God's commandments and statutes so that He may show His mercy to us.

12. God's Laws in the New Covenant

We will look at a few Scriptures to see that the new covenant requires laws, just as did the old covenant and just as laws were required before, wherefore they cannot have been done away. As we saw, God's laws existed before He spoke them from Mount Sinai. He added the old covenant to the Abrahamic covenant, because that Abraham's descendants did not keep His commandments as Abraham had (Gal. 3:19). God made this covenant with Abraham 430 years before Mount Sinai. He told Abraham to walk before Him and to be perfect, and then He would make His covenant with him. And because that Abraham kept His commandments, He therefore made the covenant with him: *And when Abram was ninety years old and nine, the LORD appeared to Abram, and said unto him, I am the Almighty God; walk before me, and be thou perfect* (Gen. 17:1). Does this sound as if God had no commandments and laws before Mount Sinai?

> *And I will make thy seed to multiply as the stars of heaven, and will give unto thy seed all these countries; and in thy seed shall all the nations of the earth be blessed; Because that Abraham obeyed my voice, and kept **my charge***

\<mishmereth\>,[22] *my commandments*
\<mitsvah\>,[23] *my statutes* **\<chuqqah\>,**[24]
and my laws **\<towrah\>**[25] (Gen. 26:4–5).

Not only the Jews, but all nations would be blessed through
this covenant that He made with Abraham 430 years before
Mount Sinai.

What commandments and laws did Abraham obey 430
years before Mount Sinai? Abraham's descendants were
already included in the covenant that God made with him
at that time: *And I will establish my covenant between me
and thee and thy seed after thee in their generations for an
everlasting \<'owlam\>*[26] *covenant, to be a God unto thee,
and to thy seed after thee* (Gen. 17:7).

The Hebrew people were in hard bondage in Egypt
and were continually breaking God's commandments. So
God delivered them out of Egypt and reminded them of
His commandments. Later He made a covenant with them,
which included the animal sacrifices and rituals to lead
them to the promised Savior. They were to keep the law
according to the letter (physical and materialistic). We can
see that Abraham's covenant and the old covenant both
required obedience to God's commandments, statutes, and
laws, just as does the new covenant, but now according to
the Spirit (circumcision of the hearts and minds), which in
many areas is much more demanding than in the days of
old. Now we are the living (continual) sacrifice of Romans
12:1, 1 John 3:16, and 1 Peter 2:5. The promise of eternal
life in the new covenant still hangs on that covenantal
promise to and through Abraham's seed, which in the new
covenant is a spiritual Israelite, the Israel of God (Gal. 6:16).
And to obtain eternal life through the promise of the new
covenant still requires keeping God's commandments: . . .
if thou wilt enter into life, keep the commandments (Matt.
19:17; also read John 14:15; Rev. 12:17; 14:12; 22:14).

In the days of old, we were not convicted as a murderer until the other person was dead, but now, if we hate our brother, we are a murderer in our heart. We can see in the Sermon on the Mount (Matt. 5–7) that the Messiah did not come to do away with the laws. He magnified them, and brought them to their fullness, as Isaiah prophesied about 600 BC (Isa. 42:21).

The new covenant surely comes with laws:

> *For this is the covenant that I will make with the house of Israel after those days, saith the Lord; I will put my laws into their mind, and write them in their hearts: and I will be to them a God, and they shall be to me a people* (Heb. 8:10; quoted directly from the Old Testament). *But this shall be the covenant that I will make with the house of Israel; After those days, saith the LORD, I will put my* **law** **<towrah>**[25] *in their inward parts, and write it in their hearts; and will be their God, and they shall be my people* (Jer. 31:33).

This was prophesied by Jeremiah about 600 BC. What laws did God have at that time? Without the law and Torah <towrah>[25], there cannot be a new covenant.

The laws of which God had Jeremiah write are the first five books of the Holy Scriptures, which are called the Torah, meaning *instructions.* It is referred to as the Pentateuch (the first five books of the Holy Scriptures) and contains the Decalogue (the Ten Commandments). These are the laws that our Savior abolished, according to Protestant doctrine. If Luther's translation of Romans 10:4 and the Protestant theological interpretation of it are correct, then there are no laws for God to put into our hearts. And God will not give His laws of love and liberty to anyone who harbors such a belief, as Peter confirms in Acts 5:32: *And we are his witnesses of these things; and so is also the Holy Ghost, whom God hath given* **to them that obey him**. Salvation is given only to them which obey Him: *And being made perfect, he became the author of eternal salvation unto all them that obey him* (Heb. 5:9).

If you truly believe that God's laws are burdensome and a yoke of bondage, then you should do whatever you have to, to not allow God to write them in your heart. And He won't, because as we have already learned, as free moral agents, He will never force you to come to Him. All you need to do is make a choice. If you truly believe that God's laws are done away, so be it; it's your choice as a free moral agent. But He does love you, wherefore He desires you to come to Him on your own free will, that you might be saved: *The Lord is not slack concerning his promise, as some men count slackness; but is longsuffering to us-ward, not willing that any should perish, but that all should come to repentance* (2 Peter 3:9). *Who will have all men to be saved, and to come unto the knowledge of the truth* (1 Tim. 2:4). He wants us to desire Him for what He is and for what He has in store for His people, not merely alone because we don't like the alternative, which is hell and death.

For a point of interest, you will not find any covenant that God has made with the Gentiles. To be included in the promises of the new covenant, the Gentiles, just like the Jews and other Israelites, must become spiritual Israelites. The Messiah was sent for the lost sheep of the house of Israel: *I am not sent but unto the lost sheep of the house of Israel* (Matt. 15:24).

God is writing (training) His laws into the hearts and minds of His people. This process begins with the giving of the Holy Spirit, through repentance and baptism, and as He stated above, it will be done to the Israelites. What happens to the Jews and the Gentiles? The answer is that no Jew, or Gentile, or any flesh-born Israelite will reap the promise of eternal life through the new covenant or see the kingdom of God unless they become spiritual Israelites. Only true Israelites will be saved and become part of the scriptural Israel of God:

> *For as many of you as have been baptized into Christ have put on Christ. There is neither Jew nor Greek, there is neither bond nor free, there is neither male nor female: for ye are all one in Christ Jesus. And if ye be Christ's, then are ye Abraham's seed, and heirs according to the promise* (Gal. 3:27–29).

Abraham's seed, after his descendant Jacob's name was changed to Israel, are Israelites: *And as many as walk according to this rule, peace be on them, and mercy, and upon the **Israel of God*** (Gal. 6:16). This is God's church, which He started a few millennia ago, and the same church that Stephen mentions in Acts 7:38, of which the same Messiah who spoke the Ten Commandments from Mount Sinai was already the Head at that time. Where did the belief come from that the Messiah abolished the old church system (which is His law and Torah), and came to start a New Testament church with the Gentiles? Through Paul?

I will add a little for those who say that the commandments of God were for the Jews only and that Paul gave the doctrine for the Gentiles. Well, I believe that we have disproved that concept, using that so-called Paul's doctrine. I call it God's Word, because it is not Paul's doctrine, as he said in his testimonies (section 5c). There were no Jews when God spoke the Ten Commandments to the children of Israel, not until the tribes were scattered in about 759 BC, which is about 732 years after they had left Egypt. (2 Kings 16:6 is the first mention of the word *Jew* in the King James Version Scriptures.) During the scattering, most of Judah's and Benjamin's tribes banded together with the Levites, and since then they have been called Jews after Judah.

God is not a respecter of persons, wherefore He made one law for all of His people:

> *For there is no iniquity with the LORD our God, nor respect of persons, nor taking of gifts* (2 Chron. 19:7). *For there is no respect of persons with God* (Rom. 2:11). *One law shall be to him that is homeborn, and unto the stranger that sojourneth among you* (Exod. 12:49). *One law and one manner shall be for you, and for the stranger that sojourneth with you* (Num. 15:16). *For there is no difference between the Jew and the Greek: for the same Lord over all is rich unto all that call upon him* (Rom. 10:12). *Where there is neither Greek nor Jew, circumcision nor uncircumcision, Barbarian, Scythian, bond nor free: but Christ is all, and in all.* (Col. 3:11; cf. Gal. 3:28; 6:16, quoted above).

And the Lord said that His Sabbath, which is one of the Ten Commandments, was made for all mankind: *And he said unto them, The sabbath was made for **man**, and not man for the sabbath. Therefore the Son of man is Lord also of the sabbath* (Mark 2:27–28). The Pharisees took pride in believing that God had made them for the Sabbath. The Messiah set them straight in this Scripture by telling them that the Sabbath was the Lord's and made for all mankind, not just for the Jew. In the Sabbath commandment, God commanded to give even the animals a rest on that day.

The Ten Commandments, which God spoke face to face, were no more for the Israelites (or Jews, as the traditional Christians call them) than for anyone else. The belief that they were for the Jews only, and that they were Moses's laws, does not hold much water, does it? *The LORD talked with you **face to face** in the mount out of the midst of the fire* (Deut. 5:4).

13. God's Laws are Eternal, and His Word is Final

There is a way which seemeth right unto a man, but the end thereof are the ways of death (Prov. 14:12).

The Messiah's words, with the authority from His Father, stated that not one iota would pass from the laws until heaven and earth pass:

> *Till heaven and earth pass, one jot or one tittle shall in no wise pass from the law, till all be fulfilled* (Matt. 5:18). *And it is easier for heaven and earth to pass, than one tittle of the law to fail* (Luke 16:17). *Heaven and earth shall pass away: but my words shall not pass away* (Luke 21:33).

According to these Scriptures, His Laws will continue for yet some time. His Word will never end. God changes not, and He cannot lie:

> *For I am the LORD, I change not* (Mal. 3:6). *Jesus Christ the same yesterday, and to day, and for ever* (Heb. 13:8). *God, that cannot lie...* (Titus 1:2). *Concerning thy testimonies,*

> *I have known of old that thou hast founded them **for ever** <`owlam>*[26] *(Ps. 119:152). I know that, whatsoever God doeth, it shall be **for ever** <`owlam>:*[26] *nothing can be put to it, nor any thing taken from it: and God doeth it, that men should fear before him (Eccl. 3:14). Every good gift and every perfect gift is from above, and cometh down from the Father of lights, with whom is **no variableness, neither shadow of turning** (James 1:17).* There is not a *shadow* of variance in the eternal God.

These are the same words our Messiah spoke in the Sermon on the Mount: *One jot or one tittle shall in no wise pass from the law . . .* (Matt. 5:18; cf. Deut. 4:2; 12:32; Rev. 22:18–19.)

> *The fear of the LORD is the beginning of wisdom: a good understanding have all they that do his commandments: His praise endureth for ever* <*`ad>*[27]*. Praise ye the LORD. Blessed is the man that feareth the LORD, that delighteth greatly in his commandments.* (Ps. 111:10–112:1; quoted from Deut. 4:6). *It is a fearful thing to fall into the hands of the living God* (Heb. 10:31).

Solomon, the wisest man ever to have lived, has a very solid piece of fail-safe advice: *Let us hear the conclusion of the whole matter: Fear God, and keep his commandments: for this is the whole duty of man* (Eccl. 12:13). If all else fails he advises, **keep the commandments**. And as he stated in 3:14, God's Word will not change!

14. Words of Wisdom

It *is better to trust in the LORD than to put confidence in
man* (Ps. 118:8). *Trust in the LORD with all thine heart;
and lean not unto thine own understanding. In all thy ways
acknowledge him, and he shall direct thy paths. Be not wise
in thine own eyes: fear the LORD, and depart from evil. It
shall be health to thy navel, and marrow to thy bones* (Prov.
3:5–8). *We ought to obey God rather than men* (Acts 5:29).
*The fear of the LORD is the beginning of wisdom: a good
understanding have all they that do his commandments: his
praise endureth for ever. Praise ye the LORD. Blessed is the
man that feareth the LORD, that delighteth greatly in his
commandments. His seed shall be mighty upon earth: the
generation of the upright shall be blessed* (Ps. 111:10–112:2).
*The fear of the LORD is the beginning of knowledge: but fools
despise wisdom and instruction* (Prov. 1:7). *The fear of the
LORD is the beginning of wisdom: and the knowledge of the
holy is understanding* (Prov. 9:10). *The fear of the LORD is
the instruction of wisdom; and before honour is humility*
(Prov. 15:33). (read also Psalms 19; 111; 112; 119.)

*Blessed is the man that walketh not in the counsel of the
ungodly, nor standeth in the way of sinners, nor sitteth in the
seat of the scornful. But his delight is in the law of the LORD;
and in his law doth he meditate day and night. And he shall*

be like a tree planted by the rivers of water, that bringeth forth his fruit in his season; his leaf also shall not wither; and whatsoever he doeth shall prosper. The ungodly are not so: but are like the chaff which the wind driveth away. Therefore the ungodly shall not stand in the judgment, nor sinners in the congregation of the righteous. For the LORD knoweth the way of the righteous: but the way of the ungodly shall perish (Ps. 1:1-6).

15. Conclusion

If you feel that some of the truths that I've revealed in this book are bit off the wall, remember this: God does not change (Mal. 3:6; Heb. 13:8; James 1:17), wherefore He cannot lie (Titus 1:2); the Scriptures do not contradict (John 10:35); all Scripture is God-breathed (2 Tim. 3:16); and we are to study and prove the Scriptures for ourselves (2 Tim. 2:15). Do it for yourself, not for me or for a preacher or for anyone, but do it for your own benefit.

One could dig deeper into this topic than we have. My prayer is that we have come to the conclusion and understanding that God has not done away with His laws. I trust that we have seen ample scriptural proof that we need not doubt that, if any Scripture seems to indicate that the laws and commandments of God have been done away, we can know for sure and with absolute certainty that we are, as carnal-minded human beings, misunderstanding that Scripture, because we do know (without excuse) that the Scriptures cannot and will not contradict themselves. I believe that we have come to the understanding that God's Word, His laws, His statutes, and His commandments are from eternity to eternity, and that they are all for His honor and glory and to our benefit. Let us not forget to praise Him for that continually, forever and ever. Amen.

My heartfelt prayer is that our merciful, loving, and gracious God and Father would reveal His truths to us and cause us to respond to His revelations in ways that are pleasing in His sight, so that He can walk with us and so that we might therefore become true disciples of our Lord and saving Messiah. May the great eternal God of heaven and earth be glorified forever. So be it.

May God bless you richly, now and forever.

Cornie Banman, Box 292, La Crete AB T0H 2H0, Canada
Phone: 780-928-3679, E-mail: cornieb@sis.net
http://corniebanman.com

God willing, my second book *'Traditional Anti-Torah Church Doctrines, The Curses of Our Fathers'* will be published by the end of 2013. Watch for updates on my website.

==============================

16. Scripture References

New Testament Quotes:	Quoted on Page:	Referenced on Page:
1 Corinthians 1:19-30		26
1 Corinthians 3:17		102
1 Corinthians 5:7	118	
1 Corinthians 5:8	78	
1 Corinthians 5:11	62	
1 Corinthians 7:19	28, 107	33, 43
1 Corinthians 10:1–14		68
1 Corinthians 10:13–14	102	37
1 Corinthians 10:14, 20–21	64	124
1 Corinthians 10:1-21		102
1 Corinthians 11:1–2	79	80
1 Corinthians 11:22-27		13
1 Corinthians 14:33	26	85
1 Corinthians 15:31	107	116
1 Corinthians 15:45–47		106
1 John 1:9	48	6
1 John 1:8–10		94
1 John 2:3–4	28, 70, 85, 87, 119	86, 94
1 John 2:6	49, 103	
1 John 2:7	119	12
1 John 2:25	41	
1 John 3:4	12, 28, 87	47, 94, 122
1 John 3:5		81
1 John 3:15	17, 28	
1 John 3:16	18	106, 120, 127
1 John 3:16–18	111	

2 Peter 2:6		12
2 Peter 2:19	3	
2 Peter 2:20–22	67	
2 Peter 3:9	129	
2 Peter 3:15–17	85	
2 Thessalonians 2:3	85	
2 Timothy 2:15	25, 89	83, 136
2 Timothy 3:15–17	25	28, 32, 136
2 Timothy 4:3–4	26, 86	69
Acts 3:13		42
Acts 3:19	47	
Acts 4:12		48
Acts 5:28–29	80	
Acts 5:29	44, 134	
Acts 5:32	46, 55, 128	
Acts 7:6	2	
Acts 7:38		130
Acts 8:9–11	53	
Acts 10:14		63
Acts 13:39	111	
Acts 14:8–19	76	
Acts 15:5	100	
Acts 15:10	2, 100	99, 100
Acts 17:11	91	
Acts 18:21	78	
Acts 19:35	77	
Acts 21:24	92	
Acts 23:6		58
Acts 26:5	58	
Acts 28:23	35	
Colossians 2:8	85	

17. Hebrew/Greek/English Definitions

1. Greek for **love** #26 agaph **agape**, ag-ah'-pay; from 25; love, i.e. affection or benevolence; specially (plural) a love-feast:-(feast of) charity(-ably), dear, love. Pages 9, 22, 44, 51, 55, 103, 106, 107, 108, 117, 120.

1a Greek for **love** #25 agapaw **agapao**, ag-ap-ah'-o; perhaps from agan (much); to love (in a social or moral sense):-(be-)love(-ed). Page 9.

1b Greek for **love** #5384 filov **philos**, fee'-los; properly, dear, i.e. a friend; actively, fond, i.e. friendly (still as a noun, an associate, neighbor, etc.):-friend. Page 9.

2 Hebrew for **Babel** #894 lbb **Babel**, baw-bel'; Babel (i.e. Babylon), including Babylonia and the Babylonian empire:-Babel, Babylon. Page 12.

3 Hebrew for **sanctify** #6942 vdq **qadash**, kaw-dash'; a primitive root; to be (causatively, make, pronounce or observe as) clean (ceremonially or morally):-appoint, bid, consecrate, dedicate, defile, hallow, (be, keep) holy(-er, place), keep, prepare, proclaim, purify, sanctify(-ied one, self), X wholly. Page 16.

4 Greek for **enmity** #2189 **echthra**, ekh'-thrah; hostility; by implication, a reason for opposition:-enmity, hatred. Page 23.

5 Greek for **subject** #5293 upotassw **hupotasso**, hoop-ot-as'-so; to obey:-be under obedience (obedient), put under, subdue unto, (be, make) subject (to, unto), be (put) in subjection (to, under), submit self unto. Page 23.

6 Greek for **law** #3551 nomov **nomos**, nom'-os; from a primary nemo (to parcel out, especially food or grazing to animals); law (through the idea of prescriptive usage), genitive case (regulation), specially, (of Moses (including the volume); also of the Gospel), or figuratively (a principle):-law. Pages 42, 43, 44, 45, 50, 51, 52, 93, 115, 116.

7 Greek for **commandment** #1785 entolh **entole**, en-tol-ay'; from 1781; injunction, i.e. an authoritative prescription:-commandment, precept. Pages 43, 44, 54, 57, 68, 81, 82, 100, 107, 115, 119.

8 Greek word for **ordinance** #1378 dogma **dogma**, dog'-mah; a law (civil, ceremonial or ecclesiastical):-decree, ordinance. Page 44.

9 Greek for **works** #2041 ergon **ergon**, er'-gon; from a primary (but obsolete) ergo (to work); toil (as an effort or occupation); by implication, an act:-deed, doing, labour, work. Pages 52, 54, 116.

10 Greek for **unrighteousness** #458 **anomia**, an-om-ee'-ah; illegality, i.e. violation of law or (genitive case) wickedness:-iniquity, X transgress(-ion of) the law, unrighteousness. Pages 62, 87, 88.

11 Greek for **commandment** #1778 entalma **entalma**, en'-tal-mah; from 1781; an injunction, i.e. religious precept:—commandment. Pages 57, 68, 81, 82, 100. *[Note that the word for commandment as translated from the Greek word 'entole' #1785 (endnote #7) is not the 'religious' precept as is 'entalma' #1778. 'Entole' distinctively prescribes to 'God's commandments, while 'entalma' distinctively prescribes to man's]*

12 Greek for **simplicity** #572 aplothv **haplotes**, hap-lot'-ace; from 573; singleness, i.e. (subjectively) sincerity (without dissimulation or self-seeking), or (objectively) generosity (copious bestowal):—bountifulness, liberal(-ity), simplicity, singleness. Page 62.

13 Greek for **unclean** #169 akayartov **akathartos**, ak-ath'-ar-tos; from 1 (as a negative particle) and a presumed derivative of 2508 (meaning cleansed); impure (ceremonially, morally (lewd) or specially, (demonic)):—foul, unclean. Page 63.

14 Greek for **ordinance** #3862 paradosiv **paradosis**, par-ad'-os-is; transmission, i.e. (concretely) a precept; specially, the Jewish traditionary law:-ordinance, tradition. Page 80.

15 Greek for **ordinance** #2937 ktisiv **ktisis**, ktis'-is; from 2936; original formation (properly, the act; by implication, the thing, literally or figuratively):-building, creation, creature, ordinance. Page 80.

16 Greek for **wicked** #113. ayesmov **athesmos**, ath'-es-mos; lawless, i.e. (by implication) criminal:-wicked. Page 85.

17 Greek for **end**: #5056 telov **telos**, tel'-os; from a primary tello (to set out for a definite point or goal); properly, the point aimed at as a limit, i.e. (by implication) the conclusion of an act or state (termination (literally, figuratively or indefinitely), result (immediate, ultimate or prophetic), purpose); specially, an impost or levy (as paid):-+ continual, custom, end(-ing), finally, uttermost. Pages 93, 115, 118.

18 Greek for **kept** #5432 frourew **phroureo**, froo-reh'-o; to be a watcher in advance, i.e. to mount guard as a sentinel (post spies at gates); figuratively, to hem in, protect:-keep (with a garrison). Page 116.

19 Greek for **end** #5055 telew **teleo**, tel-eh'-o; from 5056; to end, i.e. complete, execute, conclude, discharge (a debt):-accomplish, make an end, expire, fill up, finish, go over, pay, perform. Page 118.

20 Greek for **end** #4930 sunteleia **sunteleia**, soon-tel'-i-ah; from 4931; entire completion, i.e. consummation (of a dispensation):-end. Page 118.

21 Greek for **chasteneth** #3811 paideuw **paideuo**, pahee-dyoo'-o; from 3816; to train up a child, i.e. educate, or (by implication), discipline (by punishment):—chasten(-ise), instruct, learn, teach. Page 125.

22 Hebrew for **charge** 4931 trmvm **mishmereth**, mish-meh'-reth; watch, i.e. the act (custody), or (concr.) the sentry, the post; obj. preservation, or (concr.) safe; fig. observance, i.e. (abstr.) duty or (obj.) a usage or party:-charge, keep, or to be kept, office, ordinace, safeguard, ward, watch. Page 127.

23 Hebrew for **commandment** #4687 hwum **mitsvah**, mits-vaw'; a command, whether human or divine (collectively, the Law):-(which was) commanded(-ment), law, ordinance, precept. Page 127.

24 Hebrew for **statute** #2708 hqx **chuqqah**, khook-kaw':-appointed, custom, manner, ordinance, site, statute. Page 127.

25 Hebrew for **laws** #08451 hrwt **towrah**, to-raw'; or torah {to-raw'}; a precept or statute, especially the Decalogue or Pentateuch:-law. Pages 127, 128.

26 Hebrew for **everlasting** and **forever** #5769 Mlwe `owlam, o-lawm'; . . . time out of mind (past or future) . . . eternity . . . Eternal . . . perpetual . . . (beginning of the) world (+ without end). Pages 126, 133.

27 Hebrew for '**ad** #5703 de `**ad**, ad; from 5710; properly, a (peremptory) terminus, i.e. (by implication) duration, in the sense of advance or perpetuity (substantially as a noun, either with or without a preposition):--eternity, ever (- lasting, -more), old, perpetually, + world without end. Page 133.